# DOUBLE DUTY

## DUAL IDENTITY

Raised in an Alcoholic/Dysfunctional Family and

# FOOD ADDICTED

by Claudia Black, M.S.W., Ph.D.

ISBN No.:0-910223-16-5

**"Double Duty - Food Addicted"** Copyright © By CLAUDJA, inc
Printed in the United States of America. All Rights Reserved.
This book or parts thereof may not be reproduced in any form without written permission of the author.

1st Printing, June 1990.

**MAC PUBLISHING**
a division of CLAUDJA, inc.
5005 East 39th Avenue
Denver, CO 80207
(303) 331-0148 • Fax (303) 331-0212

To my contributors, a.k.a.
Skip, Felicia, Paul and Gloria

# ACKNOWLEDGEMENTS

I would like to express my gratitude to all of the contributors who participated in this project. While only five life stories appear in the final book I am also greatly indebted to the others who offered stories. These people displayed not only a rare courage and generosity — they reached deeply into themselves and discovered yet another level of their own recovery.

I would also like to acknowledge my professional friends who gave me feedback on various chapters throughout this series. Leslie Drozd, Ph.D.; Victoria Danzig, M.S.W.; Don Steckdaub, M.A.; Doug Braun, M.F.C.; Jill Borman; Jael Greenleaf; Ed Ellis, Ph.D.; Dana Finnegan; Emily McNally; Mel Pohl, M.D.; Skip Sauvain, M.A.; Wynn Bloch, M.A.; Wayne Smith; Betty La Porte and Sam Ryan.

Thanks to Mary McClellan, of San Francisco who worked with me on the presentation of those stories; Barbara Shor, for her copy editing. Anne Marsin for her typing and retyping that was so vital in this project; Cheryl Woodruff, the editor of the book Double Duty, from which these are edited; Jack Fahey, my husband and business partner who has read and reread every version of every chapter. He one more time walked me through this process every inch of the way.

# CONTENTS

**Chapter**                                                       **Page**

Acknowledgements

Double Duty . . . . . . . . . . . . . . . . . . . . . . . . . . 1

Food Addiction - Dual Identity . . . . . . . . . . . . . . . . 6

Adult Child Issues . . . . . . . . . . . . . . . . . . . . . . . 11

Life Stories . . . . . . . . . . . . . . . . . . . . . . . . . 14

    Growing Up Years . . . . . . . . . . . . . . . . . . . . . . 16

The Role Of Food . . . . . . . . . . . . . . . . . . . . . . 41

Adulthood and Recovery . . . . . . . . . . . . . . . . . . . 49

Recovery Considerations . . . . . . . . . . . . . . . . . . . 74

    Primary Addiction . . . . . . . . . . . . . . . . . . . . . 74

    Multiple Addictions . . . . . . . . . . . . . . . . . . . . 74

    Shame . . . . . . . . . . . . . . . . . . . . . . . . . . 76

    Incest . . . . . . . . . . . . . . . . . . . . . . . . . . . 76

    Feelings . . . . . . . . . . . . . . . . . . . . . . . . . 77

    Control . . . . . . . . . . . . . . . . . . . . . . . . . . 78

    Isolation . . . . . . . . . . . . . . . . . . . . . . . . . 78

    Perfectionism . . . . . . . . . . . . . . . . . . . . . . . 79

Appendixes:

Self Help Programs And National Organizations

Are You A Food Addict?

Original Laundry List — Adult Children of Alcoholics

Progression Chart

Do You Have The Disease of Alcoholism?


Other Books By Claudia Black

# DOUBLE DUTY

While there has been a proliferation of books about Young and Adult Children of Alcoholics it is important to recognize that the Children of Alcoholics movement is still in its infancy. We are only now beginning to understand the complexity of the trauma within the dysfunctional family systems so many Adult children have experienced and the ways this has compromised their adulthood.

Over the past few years thousands of Adult Children have begun their process of self-healing. There have been many wonderful miracles. Yet, as I watched people moving through their recovery, I have also seen many individuals hit a baffling impenetrable wall that halted their progress. There seemed to be a missing link or another piece to the puzzle. A very big piece of what I believe causes such blockage is the experience that I call **Double Duty.**

I define double duty as the intensified life experiences of ACOAs who have contended, not only with family alcoholism or dysfunction, but have also dealt with an additional set of circumstances that have profoundly affected their lives and their recovery. Many Adult Children belittle and criticize themselves for not moving through recovery as easily or as speedily as others they know. When ACOAs are unable to work through the recovery process with as much ease or speed as they would like, it is often because of their need to identify and address multiple issues in recovery. People who have multiple issues often have an additional need to protect themselves, and this may be why they do not connect with self-help groups or the therapy process as quickly as others.

One of the key premises of the ACOA recovery process is putting the past behind us. That only occurs when the truth of one's experience is acknowledged. Up to this time in the evolution of the ACOA movement, the stores told — and as a result the issues addressed — have tended to be very generalized. This stage of emphasizing the experiences all ACOA have in common has been incredibly valuable. However, now that many Adult Children have spent several years in recovery form their ACOA issues, I believe it is time to explore how Adult Children differ from each other. And that difference is what **Double Duty** is all about.

This book describes in detail the process the child experiences in an alcoholic family. It also examines the special problems of multiple issues — which I call **"Double Duty/Dual Identity"** (DD/DI) — that these Adult Children face and the step-by-step process of their recovery. We can no longer continue to apply generic recovery programs to all ACOAs. While General recovery information is most often what one needs to focus on in early recovery, in time an individual's unique life situation has to be and deserves to be addressed. By refusing to look at the specifics of an individual's experiences we can inadvertently trivialize the purpose of the entire movement.

The concept of **Double Duty** is not meant to encourage people to use their differentness to keep others away or to resist new opportunities. I believe we must first see our communalities, and humble then comfort ourselves in the recognition that we are not unique. Although, we suffered separately, we have not suffered alone. Only after we have acknowledged this common ground should we undertake to explore what may have been unique in our experiences.

There are many reasons for differences among Adult Children. Birth order affects children differently, sex role expectations affect children differently. Who the chemically dependent parent is and the dynamics of how co-dependency shows itself create differences among ACOAs. Many areas merit exploration, but I have chosen certain areas that warrant deeper exploration for the Adult Child in the recovery process. It is my hope that the areas explored in **Double Duty** will offer a conceptual model upon which others may build.

Double duty exists when a child has one major trauma-inducing dynamic in the family and there exists an additional dynamic that reinforces the consequences though added trauma or complexity.

For instance, if there is a terminally ill sibling in a child's family, growing up can be quite traumatic. But is does not have to create a lifelong trauma if there is a healthy family system to help the surviving child respond to the situation. However, put the set of circumstances in an alcoholic or otherwise troubled family, and the child involved will suffer many long-lasting effects from both issues. This is what I mean by a double duty situation.

In order to endure such trauma and added complexity — simply in order to survive — this child has to toughen up much more than other children. In adulthood, such survivors are likely to have their defenses much more rigidly in place and their emotions very hardened.

I envision the double duty COA as a small child, hunched over, dragging unwieldy boxes and overflowing bags of trauma, when suddenly a dump truck comes roaring up and adds another load of pain.

By contrast, **Dual Identity** is a special form of **Double Duty** in which one has at least two equally commanding aspects to one's identity — such as being a COA and a person of color or being a COA and gay or lesbian. It is like looking into a two-sided mirror and seeing one image of yourself on one side and an equally real but different image on the other side. Although the images are different, they are invisibly enmeshed. This leaves Adult Children even more confused about who they are and what is most important in their lives.

For the purpose of Adult Child recovery it is important to recognize that as an ACOA, there may be other, equally significant aspects of your identity that need to be recognized and addressed — beyond those of having been raised in a chemically dependent family — in order to experience a full recovery.

**Double Duty/Dual Identity** are examples of the synergistic effect of multiple-core issues that many Adult Children experience. The added dynamics of **Double Duty/Dual Identity** often force children to protect themselves even further. As a result, issues such as not trusting, not feeling, fear of losing control, and an overwhelming sense of shame are experienced even more deeply. It then becomes much more difficult for the afflicted ACOA to ask for help or to feel any hope. Very often the feeling of being overwhelmed by emotion or of having frozen emotions greatly impedes the ability to connect with a recovery process.

There are many people who know they are Adult Children, who know resources are available, who may even truly want to change their lives — yet always find that something seems to get in the way when they try to connect with a helping resource or try to stay involved once they've found that resource. There are others who are so powerfully defended against their pain that their level of denial is too strong for them even to recognize that their lives could be better. Still others become stuck in the process of recovery and "spin their wheels." These are often the DD/DI people. In this book we will explore the phenomena of being raised in an alcoholic/dysfunctional family and being food addicted.

*"What I learned from growing up in an alcoholic family was that the world was a painful and scary place. Food became my means of escaping from those feelings."*

Adult Child

# FOOD ADDICTION — DUAL IDENTITY

Compulsive overeating, bulimia, and anorexia are all aspects of the same disease — food dependency. Compulsion, obsession, and denial are the common denominators that weave through these dependencies.

Most people who are compulsive overeaters are not obese. They are much more likely to be chronically ten to twenty pounds overweight and preoccupied compulsively with food and body size. Compulsive overeaters react to sugars and starches in extreme ways. They experience mood changes ranging from euphoric highs to irritability, from feeling nurtured and comforted to being in a mental frenzy or stupor.

The most visible eating disorder is overeating that results in obesity. Although this book discusses the psychological factors that influence extreme overeating and create obesity, it must be remembered that under some circumstances, obesity can be caused by purely physiological conditions. There are rare metabolic exceptions and genetic considerations that create obesity. Nonetheless, whatever the reasons for obesity, the psychological, social, and physical consequences are severe. It has been well established that obese people have shorter life spans due to strokes, heart attacks, and arteriosclerosis.

Bulimia is a second form of eating disorder. Bulimics overeat, typically in binges, and then they purge through laxative use, diuretic (water pills) abuse, or by forced vomiting and compulsive exercise. Bulimics, like most compulsive overeaters, tend to be within ten to twenty pounds of average weight. The binge and purge cycle of bulimia closely parallels the highs and crashes that drug addicts know so well. First comes the euphoric high of the binge, then comes the drastic expulsion of the food.

Anorexia is a third type of eating disorder. Anorexics are obsessed with not eating. They may even have an unnatural fear of food.

Anorexics starve themselves — a compulsion that is often reinforced by the biological euphoria produced by starvation.

Starving and binge/purging can produce serious medical problems ranging from dehydration and disturbances in the body's fluid and mineral balance to irreversible liver damage, diabetes, hypoglycemia, heart attacks, and kidney failure. In some cases, gorging and forced vomiting rupture the stomach or esophagus, causing infections and death.

Whatever the form of the disorder, eating takes on a compulsive quality. People feel driven to eat or to starve as though they had no choice. This compulsion effectively blocks awareness of their feelings and serves to distract them from anxiety and from unpleasant feelings and memories. When people are frightened of their feelings, or experience painful feelings, excessive food intake or extreme food deprivation helps them deny and repress the pain.

Overeaters also indulge in food when they're happy and joyful. Many overeat as a reward. Food can become the answer to any feeling.

People who feel poorly about themselves often use food for solace. Those with low self-esteem and a tendency to isolate themselves are much more likely to regard food as a friend. Food nurtures. Food anesthetizes.

People who are overburdened with shame, who have come to believe they are defective or bad, often find that compulsive overeating is the best way to assuage this pain. However, it can also be a form of self-punishment — a consciously abusive act. Overeating fuels the bulimic's sense of shame, while purging is sometimes an attempt to alleviate even greater shame. The anorexic may unconsciously be looking for a way to become invisible, to disappear.

Bulimics and anorexics often feel revulsion about their bodies and starve or purge themselves as punishment. This revulsion may be fed by a distorted perception of their bodies. They often see themselves as fat when they are quite thin or of average body weight. Overeaters may be repulsed by their bodies and overeat in response to their feelings of futility and powerlessness. Yet overeaters usually have distorted perceptions, too. Most often they believe they're smaller than they actually are, yet some see themselves as larger than they are. Early on, they all quit looking in the mirror. And they all tend to be disconnected from their bodies.

Both overeaters and undereaters have a great deal of difficulty verbalizing their internal experiences. This is because they're removed from both their feelings and their needs. They don't recognize the internal and external cues and signals that serve as indicators of their true needs.

People with eating disorders also display a significant amount of passive-aggressive behavior. They often appear compliant and passive on the outside while feeling and often denying their deep anger and resentment inside. They then act out that hostility against their own bodies.

These are people who struggle constantly with issues of powerlessness and control. Often they experience themselves as totally helpless in a very frightening world. The overeating may symbolize their feelings of being out of control. It certainly reinforces the powerlessness.

Bulimics and anorexics often have major issues around perfectionism. They have bought into the notion that if they can control their exterior, they can become more acceptable in their interior, where they often feel fear, hurt, loneliness, and shame. The control they experience with food may be the only control they feel they have in their lives.

In Western culture, food is largely associated with nurturance. Children are routinely given food to soothe or as a reward. We are programmed from a young age to use food to fill our emptiness. Children literally hunger for love and approval, and when that is missing in their lives, food often becomes an alternative.

Eating disorders are referred to as *"diseases of isolation."* Those with eating disorders tend to have spent a tremendous amount of time in isolation filled with loneliness. As children they often experienced being alone as being abandoned. They internalized this feeling of abandonment as proof that they were not of value. Food became a substitute for human interaction. When parents weren't available, food provided the solace. But the fact that the hurt feelings weren't assuaged went unnoticed. Additionally, much of the behavior that fed their disorder was secretive, which created even greater feelings of loneliness and shame.

Eating disorders, particularly obesity and anorexia, can also be a way of calling attention to oneself — a way of expressing anger and rage; a way of rebelling and acting out. Compulsive overeating is often a way of pushing people away. Especially when one has been sexually abused, being overweight may be an attempt to keep people away to prevent further abuse. For anorexics, starving is a way of attracting attention while still keeping people at a distance.

It is important to recognize that in every eating disorder, the relationship with food becomes addictive. And, as with any addiction, the relationship to the addiction becomes the major focus in the person's life. Food addiction is much like any other substance and process addiction. It moves through

- Loss of control
- Denial
- Increased dependence
- Change in tolerance
- Impaired thinking
- Preoccupation with and the control of the addictive substance
- Manipulation of one's environment to obtain the desired effects
- Lying
- Obsession
- Guilt and remorse
- Physical deterioration

# ADULT CHILD ISSUES

Research has clearly demonstrated that Children of Alcoholics are more prone to become chemically dependent. However, only recently have we begun to recognize that other compulsive and addictive behaviors can also be attributed to being raised in an alcoholic family.

Adult Children often routinely medicate the pain of their past and of their present with food, becoming overeaters in the process. They fluctuate between the need to be in total control of their food intake and feeling totally out of control. Their poor self-esteem, often coupled with self-hate, contributes to self-destructive behavior that manifests itself in overeating, binging, purging, and starving. Once they are into these distinctive patterns of self-abuse, they shroud themselves in shame, and their need to hide and keep secrets becomes even more pronounced.

The Adult Child characteristics that appear to be integral to those with eating addictions are:
- Control and powerlessness
- Perfectionism
- Repressed feelings — particularly anger
- Shame
- Needs

**Control and Powerlessness.** Children need to experience a sense of physical and psychological safety in their lives. They need primary caretakers to set healthy limits, to provide nurturance and support, and they need to have expectations that are appropriate for their age and experience. When parental figures do not establish the appropriate parameters and levels of control that produce a sense of safety, children accurately feel profound loss and powerlessness. They often act out that powerlessness, or they seek ways of controlling their lives by any means necessary. COAs struggle with their powerlessness on an ongoing basis. For many Adult Children, the intake or lack of intake of food is the only place in which their power lies. They seek control by attempting to manipulate what they have the power to affect. By finding the areas they can control, bulimics and anorexics learn to exert control and literally hang on for dear life. Overeaters also overfuel their bodies in an attempt to feel that they have some say over what they do.

**Perfectionism.** COAs often seek perfectionism in an attempt to be in control and/or mask shame. Sometimes areas they can affect are so limited, their only control rests with their bodies. Their preoccupation with needing to look good is often an external way of protecting themselves and protecting their family. If they look good, their problems and those of their families will remain hidden from others. No one will be able to see beyond the false exterior to the real chaos and sickness in their lives. Starving and purging are clearly actions in pursuit of perfection.

**Feelings.** COAs are people who live with chronic fear, loneliness, hurt, and disappointment. They experience resentment and anger. They live with embarrassment and guilt — often believing that there's something terribly wrong with them. Theirs becomes a life of shame. Food offers solace, and it also deadens the pain.

**Shame.** Adult Children were raised with physical and emotional abandonment. They did not get the approval, the attention, or the love they needed. Very early they came to believe there was something extremely defective inside them, that they could never be good enough. If there had also been physical or sexual abuse, they experienced being treated as objects, not as people. These were major acts of boundary violation. Food anesthetizes the pain of the growing-up years and fills the emptiness that comes with past and present shame. Anorexics or bulimics often seek to escape from their feelings of inadequacy by driving themselves to perfect their bodies by starving and purging. Overeaters seek to compensate for their early abandonment by nurturing themselves with food.

**Needs.** These dysfunctional families are alcohol-and drug-centered rather than child-centered; these children learn that adults are not going to be available to attend to their needs on a consistent basis. They also find out that they can't even meet their own needs because they are just children. As a result, they learn to repress and minimize their needs, often becoming so good at it that they cease to be able to recognize their own needs. This behavior often brings on depression — a valid response to years of not having their needs met. But their depression makes them even more socially and emotionally isolated. Compulsive eating is a way of attending to those unrecognized needs; as well as a response to the depression that is fueled as a result of needs not being met.

# LIFE STORIES

Why is it some children develop eating disorders, others become chemically dependent, and still others develop different compulsive disorders? That's difficult to answer. However, once you look at an individual's history, the reasons usually become more obvious.

Some eating disorders reflect physiological predispositions. Just as there may be a chemical tendency toward alcohol and other drug addictions, there may also be a predisposition toward obesity. With eating disorders, you will often see that the adult was a child who tended to be more socially and emotionally isolated. Compulsive eating is a way of attending to those unrecognized needs; as well as a response to the depression that is fueled as a result of needs not being met.

In the following stories, you will see that food played a significant role from a very young age. Food was the mother's way of nurturing when she was bankrupt of other emotional resources. Dysfunctional parents often become preoccupied with food and body size and image in their need to control. For some, chronic childhood illnesses fed isolation, and food provided nurturance in times of stress.

The four Adult Children who are sharing their stories have had to struggle with eating disorders. Clearly, anorexia and bulimia are predominantly female disorders. Males tend to fall into compulsive overeating that sometimes results in obesity. I've split the stories equally between men and women because as more men are entering Adult Child recovery, many of them are identifying compulsive overeating as a response to their Adult Child issues. These life stories illustrate how overeating, starving, and purging became responses to being raised in chemically dependent homes. Three of our life stories are about compulsive overeaters.

Skip was dangerously obese all through childhood — his top weight was four hundred pounds. Yet, for fifteen years now he has maintained an average weight of one hundred and seventy pounds.

At the age of fourteen, Gloria came close to dying of anorexia. In her twenties she physically recovered to confront yet another level of recovery.

Felicia struggled with the meaning of food all during childhood, then became a compulsive overeater and finally a bulimic. Gloria and Felicia reflect family histories of sexual abuse. Felicia and Skip are alcoholics.

Paul struggles with being *"husky"* as a child, and twenty five to fifty pounds overweight as an adult until he recovered in Overeaters Anonymous. The grandchild of an alcoholic, Paul was raised by two Adult Children. His story is amazingly representative because so many people with eating disorders come from third-generation alcoholic families. His parents' Adult Child issues played a strong role in the development of Paul's eating disorder.

# GROWING-UP YEARS

---

## SKIP

Age: 40
Mother: Co-dependent
Father: Alcoholic
Birth Order: Youngest of four
Raised: Indiana
Socioeconomic Status: Middle class

---

**SKIP:**

*"My father drank alcoholically until I was five years old. Then he stopped and went to Alcoholics Anonymous for one year. After that, he was a dry drunk with no emotional recovery. Although I have very little memory of my life from the time I was three until I was nine, I do have a sense that his 'not drinking' was so fragile that none of us in the family could breathe for fear he'd start drinking again.*

*"He'd come home from work, get on the couch, eat dinner alone at the coffee table, nap, and then go to bed. I remember feeling fearful, as if I needed to keep a lid on myself in order to avoid contact with him."*

Skip describes his father as being abstinent but with no emotional recovery. That occurs for various reasons, but the most common is that the alcoholic doesn't stay involved in an active recovery program. This is what happened to Skip's father. He went to AA for one year and then "stayed in control." He controlled himself by not drinking, and he controlled his family with his silence.

The fact that Skip cannot remember events from the time he was three until he was nine implies that his experiences of that time were overwhelmingly frightening. Sometimes the traumatic events that damage a child's sense of security and self-worth are overt — such as physical abuse. But the trauma is not so blatant in Skip's situation. Although silence is not often regarded as a source of significant trauma in a child's life, Skip and his siblings were subjected to their father's punishing silence. He was not just a quiet man — he was blatantly rejecting. His menacing silence was emotional torture to all the family members. A child developing a sense of identity and self-worth raised in an emotionally cold family internalizes the feeling that he must have caused this coldness. There must be something deeply wrong with him, something that makes people not want to respond to him.

Skip's description of *"keeping a lid on"* himself is an accurate metaphor for many children of troubled families. He needed to keep a lid on his feelings, on his emotional self. But, as a consequence, he couldn't keep a lid on the food. His need to control all his feelings manifested itself in his being controlling with food.

Skip's mother was a nurse. Since she worked the 11 P.M. to 7 A.M. shift, she had very little contact with Skip's father.

*"I rarely saw them talk. Mother was nurturing and caring, but she also remained quiet and isolated. She worked very hard at her career, at home, and at church. I always knew she cared for me, loved me. But I also knew that she was controlled by Dad."*

At dinnertime, Skip's dad was served his meal by his wife at the living room coffee table, in front of the television set. The four kids were served at the kitchen table.

*"We sat down, ate, and left. Any talk was negative, derogatory, caustic. We hurled our hurt at each other."*

Skip's mom didn't sit at the table, she just kept moving about, doing things. In time, three of the four children ate themselves into obesity. Skip's sister and one of his brothers were also over two hundred pounds by their late adolescence.

Skip's mother was a co-dependent. Her own sense of powerlessness had to be severe for her to keep silent about her children's obesity — as both a mother and a health professional.

Although Skip remembers his mother as warm and kind, he still felt a sense of emotional abandonment as she continued her downhill spiral into helplessness. Yet although Skip knew that something was wrong with his family, he was unable to identify it.

*"My dad didn't talk to me at all, and my mother wouldn't acknowledge that there was anything wrong. But my life was filled with this engulfing terribleness — and I thought it was me."*

Skip was screaming inside for someone to say something. This is the *"Don't talk"* rule taken literally.

*"I wanted my father to tell me there was something wrong. I wanted him to tell me it was his fault. I wanted to hear it was not my fault. Later, as I got older I needed him to tell me he was proud of me. I didn't get any of those things.*

*"My home atmosphere was very frozen. I couldn't identify my feelings at that time, but I was constantly filled with the thought that whatever was wrong was my fault. I knew that we were all on our own in this family. My siblings and I were part of the family group, but each of us was alone."*

Skip had trouble in school, beginning in the second grade when he developed a 20 percent hearing loss.

*"School was a horror for me. It was only the occasional kind gesture from a teacher that would make me feel as if I could cope at all. When I developed my hearing problems, which were accompanied by severe headaches and infections, I discovered the pleasure of being home during the day, minus my father, and the peaceful solitude that brought. While my frequent absences also increased my sense of being out of place at school, what felt best to me was to be home during the day alone. It felt safe."*

Even after his hearing problems were corrected, Skip continued to seek the safety of his solitude by feigning illness and staying home from school. This is when his eating began to take on emotional overtones.

*"I would frequently order sweets from the milkman, and I continued in this pattern for years. Eating and television were my friends, and there was a woman on a local talk show who became my mother/mentor."*

There was Skip, home alone watching television, finding comfort in his television friends, while the shows and commercials subtly, if not blatantly, reinforced the idea of food as a primary caretaker. Family shows such as Leave It to Beaver, Ozzie and Harriet, or, more recently, The Brady Bunch, demonstrating familial love, connectedness, and happy times with healthy eating — interspersed with "M'm M'm good!" commercial invitations to eat — had to make Skip even hungrier.

Skip's solitude at home, coupled with his sense of differentness, kept him from making friends until high school. His relationship with his siblings were typical of an alcoholic family.

*"My next oldest brother and I were close. I was less alone because of him. I do have a sense of his being on my side at times. My oldest brother was absent most of the time, mostly because he was very involved in sports. But I was also afraid of him because I didn't know him; he was a stranger to me.*

*"It was my sister, the oldest, who was my hero. She cleaned the house, made straight A's in school, and took care of me when I was young. She was the one who really raised me. Most of the nurturing I experienced came from her."*

Skip weighed two hundred and twenty five pounds by the time he was ten, which made him physically very different from the other children. His physical size alone would have put a distance between him and others. But he was also a COA — and most of them, regardless of size, walk through childhood feeling different and separate from others.

Nevertheless, Skip began to look outside the family for support and companionship.

*"There were many kids in my neighborhood, and they became important to me. I remember that I was always giving and doing for them, frequently buying them things and being a chameleon to their needs. This was where my main nurturing came from. Nurturing from taking care of others was a very early lesson for me."*

It is a common story to hear of fat children giving their peers money — buying them things — in hopes of securing friendships. There is such a stigma in our society associated with being fat that few children want to be friends with a fat child.

Yet, all children need and want friends. A sense of belonging is vital to a child's self-esteem. Skip was caught in the middle of a dilemma. He was struggling with being in a dysfunctional family where he felt no sense of belonging, and also with having no sense of belonging among his peers because he was a fat child. The need to buy friendships makes sense when one feels unworthy and inadequate.

However, Skip did have two close childhood friends. Because he was so fat at such a young age, the buddies he acquired early on became long-term friends — he was unable to make new ones as he got older. But, as friends sometimes do, in adolescence Skip lost one of them to new and different interests. And this loss was directly connected to his weight.

*"In high school, when my first friend became interested in girls, I felt left out. I was fat. I knew I couldn't compete in that world."*

Already struggling with school — and life — Skip lost his one remaining friend to a fatal car accident when they were in high school.

*"I was so unsupported and so unable to cope with my grief that I dropped out of school for a while. Ultimately it took me six years to finish high school. By this point I weighed four hundred pounds, which greatly added to my sense of inferiority."*

The death of a dear friend at any age is a major loss. But to lose one's only close friend as a teenager is even more difficult. There is the sadness, the anger, the loneliness, the sense of abandonment. But there are also the existential questions of life and death: *"Is dying painful?" "What is death?" "How did my friend feel about me?"* The level of pain is overwhelming, and a child has no way of knowing if it will ever end.

Skip had nowhere to take his pain. Nowhere to find solace — except in food.

The compulsiveness of his eating may or may not have been conscious. Skip may have been so disconnected from his emotional self that the pain may not have even registered emotionally. Yet it is at this time that he lost all control of his eating.

When Skip describes his family, it is with an eerie calm. It's as if he slowly and quietly gained his four hundred pounds without anyone's noticing. Yet four hundred pounds is a violent attack against one's body. It's difficult to imagine that one could launch such an offensive with no one in the family paying him any attention.

Skip was aware of feeling unremitting self-hate.

*"I would constantly tell myself I was 'no good'; that I was a terrible person."*

Most of Skip's conscious self-hatred had to do with the family environment. He was totally detached from his body image.

*"When I was very young I told myself that as long as I stayed under two hundred pounds I'd be okay. By sixth grade I had passed that. But I let it pass without much recognition. I would stand in the mirror and only see myself from the head up. I didn't see my lower body at all. I would get obsessed with my hair. I had to make sure my hair was perfect, that it was combed and sprayed. If my hair was okay then I was okay.*

By the time Skip was sixteen, his father had begun drinking again — beer on weekends. He continued this until a year before his death.

Slowly, Skip moved emotionally into adulthood — under a cloud of sadness, with an inner core of hate and fear toward his father. Food quieted the anger and comforted the sadness.

*"I was aware of nothing but an intense, overwhelming sadness. I would feel very sad in response to television shows, movies, and the stories that I would read. I can remember sometimes locking myself in the bathroom with some sad story and sobbing.*

*"In addition to the sadness, I had a lot of anger. It was a conscious, internal hatred of my father that came through frequently. But basically, it was as if I were in a functional coma all those years."*

---

# GLORIA

Age: 26
Mother: Co-dependent
Father: Pill addicted
Birth order: Oldest of three
Raised: Northeastern city
Socioeconomic: Middle class

---

Gloria was very blatantly affected by several generations of alcoholism in her family. This meant that her parents had unacknowledged Adult Child issues of their own, which may have led to her father's chemical dependency.

**GLORIA:**

*"Many of my memories of my maternal grandfather are of his being sloppily, happily drunk at our many family parties. As a kid I may not have been bothered by this, but as I grew older I was annoyed by his messy speech and slobbering kisses. My mother and grandmother both denied for years that he had any problem. The women in my family are supreme nurturers/victims/deniers/martyrs. The men are fostered, protected, and made into gods."*

Gloria's paternal grandfather was also an alcoholic and very abusive. One of the still existing family secrets is that Gloria's father and his siblings were all chronically sexually abused by their father.

Many times, as a young man, Gloria's father had had to knock out his father when he was on a drunken rampage. Out of the violence and pain of his own upbringing, Gloria's father developed a strong vision of what a family ought to be. In the end, he became a controlling, tyrannical, pill-addicted autocrat.

*"I didn't know that it was pills that were making my dad the way he was. I really never thought about why. I was just too scared. By the time I was born, my dad was already taking prescription medications. He kept the pills beside his bed in a drawer. Once, when I asked him about them, my mother clearly let me know I was not to tell my father that I knew about the pills. It was as if I was bad or wrong for seeing them. After she told me not to tell my father, she told me harshly: 'Get out of this room.' I understood it was a subject that was never again to be spoken about."*

Gloria learned early in life that she should never do anything to disturb her father. Underneath his "master of control" demeanor, there was always the silent threat of violence.

*"My mother taught me that, at all costs, I should never do anything to hurt my father or make him angry. I lived in constant fear of his awful silence that could, at the most unexpected moment, flare into red-faced rage. I have a mental image of myself in a crouch, like a dog that looks up pleadingly, hoping not to be beaten but expecting it, hoping to please the master but knowing it will never happen. The master will not, cannot, be pleased."*

Every person in this book has had to respond to issues of control by their parents. For Skip and Gloria, parental control is perpetrated on the family in silence. The father's extreme silence had the power to instill immobilizing fear into all of the other family members. The *"Don't talk"* rule was enforced through silence.

As with many COAs, Gloria's feelings toward her father were very conflicted. He often spent time with her and gave her treats. But he was also unpredictable in his behavior toward her.

*"My early years were spent both adoring and dreading my father. When I was very young, before I reached puberty, we would spend a good deal of time together, taking long walks, digging for fossils, watching Godzilla and Dracula movies. My father was the 'good guy,' the one who bought me Twinkies and soda, the one who spent money.*

*"But I would also get these terrible insults from my father. They were always delivered with a laugh. He'd tell me I was fat, ugly, and stupid. He would tease me incessantly. If I cried he'd laugh. If I got angry, he'd laugh. Finally, I decided never to show my hurt again."*

When a parent is addicted to prescription pills, a child has greater confusion about their parents' usually hurtful and erratic moods and behaviors. Because children are less likely to relate the use of pills to their parents' behavior and the mood in the home, they are even more likely than most COAs to believe they are responsible for the hurtful feelings, that there must be something wrong with them. Shame begins early.

In these cases, the children often find the nonchemically dependent parent to be the *"heavy."* The chemically dependent parent may be easier to manipulate, may simply be absent, or at times may seem more fun or likable than the other parent.

*"My mom was set up as the 'spoil sport,' the bad guy, the heavy. She was frugal — but I thought she was mean and stingy. She was careful about our eating well — but I thought her very disappointing as a mom. Other kids' mothers gave them sweets at lunch. I got an apple and maybe a plain oatmeal cookie."*

It is possible that Gloria's mother's caution about food was her way of being the *"good mother"* or the *"perfect mother."* As her husband progressed in his illness, she had an even greater need to be *"good"* or *"perfect."* Her *"goodness"* was also a way of being in control. She demonstrated her *"goodness"* in other ways as well.

*"To me, my mother appeared to be an extremely strong and overwhelmingly good person. I knew I could never be as unaffected, as noble, as unselfish, as she was. So I gave up my will to her. When*

*we'd go clothes shopping, I'd let her choose my clothes. I would express no opinion at all, although I seldom liked the clothes she picked out."*

Gloria eloquently describes what occurs for many COAs — they lose themselves in someone else. This is the beginning of her becoming invisible.

Gloria's best memories are with her brother Bobby, who is two years younger. Bobby was the funny, outgoing one. Although he had a violent temper, he usually kept it hidden. Most of the time he was affectionate and demonstrative. Gloria was quieter, less social, more reserved.

*"Bobby and I played many imaginative games together with a whole troop of Christmas elves. We even took the trouble to divide the troop into two branches of the same family. It would take us hours to name the elves and then identify their family relationships. This was almost more important than starting the game. We shared a bedroom for many years, and we'd lie awake at night playing games and talking.*

*"One of my most poignant memories is of something that happened when we were both still in grade school. As we got ready for bed, Bobby wanted to kiss me good night. But I wouldn't let him; I refused to let him touch me. I had always hated being touched and to touch. But Bobby was always very affectionate, as was my mother. My mother was pleading with me to give Bobby a good night kiss. Bobby was crying, saying that I didn't love him anymore.*

*"I lay on the bed, staring at the ceiling, 'knowing,' with the same awful certainty that I would later feel about eating food, that I could not kiss him — that if I had to kiss him, I would die. I would somehow cease to be. I didn't cry; I didn't feel anything about Bobby's pain."*

Gloria had been able to let others know her physical boundaries nonverbally. But with Bobby she had to muster the strength to speak to her beloved brother. It is difficult to fully understand what touch meant to Gloria — but it clearly was frightening to her. She has no doubts about her love for this brother. For her to reject him in this manner meant this was her last stand of physically pushing people away.

Although Gloria has no memory of any sexual molestation, her father had been an incest victim — a fact that his wife wasn't aware of until twenty years after their marriage. Gloria described her father as very undemonstrative physically. He wouldn't let others touch him and wouldn't touch others.

*"He refused kisses, he'd push you away, move his head; you couldn't touch him."*

It is possible that Gloria needed to define her physical space in a manner that couldn't include others. She was responding to her lack of psychological safety — a chronic fear of some unknown rage. Her father provided the modeling — no touching.

In school, Gloria was one of the "smart ones." She had a few special friends whom she would play with, other girls who were also good students.

*"Grammar school was largely an unpleasant experience for me. My good memories of that time have to do with after-school activities. My family lived in an apartment, but my friends all lived in houses. I loved going to their homes because there was a good deal of privacy and often a yard to play in.*

*"By seventh and eighth grades, there was a lot of drinking going on at parties. I was never a part of the 'tough' crowd. My friends and I were the ones most often tortured and teased by them. I never dated or drank. I wore glasses and braces and was very shy around boys. I spent my eight years at that school in fear — of both the students and the teachers."*

Although Gloria continued to excel academically in high school, her sense of being an outsider became even stronger.

Solitude was something that offered comfort to Gloria. But in this solitude she also discovered the isolation that would soon lead to her eating disorder.

*"I spent a great deal of time alone. On Friday nights, my favorite thing to do was sit at my desk, writing page after page of stories about girls my own age going on dates or learning about the facts of life. I also read lots of poetry and wrote verses myself, all of which rhymed. It wasn't until I was in high school and discovered the Beatles' lyrics that I started to experiment with 'free verse' and began writing more imaginative, less narrative poetry.*

*"In many ways, books saved me. Books gave me a world more real to me than the one in which I lived. I chose books for the fantasy and the challenges they offered me. I wasn't just a bookworm; I was a book vulture."*

Part of Gloria's fantasy life centered around her image of herself as a caretaker.

*"I would create a scene and then enter it. Usually there would be one or two girls, a few years younger than me, girls I knew by sight at school. I would be the 'mother/guardian' of those girls, and they would always be weak or helpless in some way, either physically frail or in some sort of trouble. I would order their world, keep it in check, and protect them."*

Her fantasy was soon to become real — although she was the one who would be physically frail and in trouble. Her *"trouble"* was the end result of her trying to protect herself, of putting her world in order, of holding everything in check.

*"In my freshman year of high school I must have heard the inevitable talk about diets. Girls that age are obsessed with how their bodies look. On some level something must have clicked: 'Ah, yes! Diet yourself to nothing! Martyr yourself. Starve yourself for attention!'*

*"I have no memory of making a decision to diet. But the following summer, when I was working at a day camp for the mentally retarded, I began to control my eating. Soon I was eating very little.*

*"From September of that year to January of the next I went from one hundred and five pounds to seventy four. I was so physically weak*

*I couldn't walk to school. I had lost nearly all of my hair. I was in such pain from the strain on my muscles that my mother had to spend hours rubbing my back. That was the onset of my anorexia."*

Gloria's story is typical of many people with eating disorders. They are very disconnected — not only from their bodies, but also from their feelings and from any insights. Gloria had very little control over her life; her mother even picked out her clothes. She describes walking in her mother's saintly shadow as she is subjected to cruel teasing by her father. At home and at school, she always felt like an outsider. Self-starvation was a clear cry for help from a young girl who was dying on the inside.

---

## PAUL

Age: 43
Mother: Adult Child
Father: Adult Child
Birth Order: Oldest of two
Raised: Midwest and California
Socioeconomic Status: Working class

---

Paul was born within a year of his parents' marriage. All the time he was growing up, he kept getting the message that, because of him, the family had been burdened with increased responsibility and financial problems. He always felt as though he had to make up for his early arrival.

At a very young age, Paul was expected to respond emotionally like an adult.

**PAUL:**
*"I came into life immediately having to excuse my existence."*

In addition to obviously arriving earlier than planned, Paul was also a sick child. He had major health problems — rheumatic fever, pneumonia, chronic asthma.

*"I was told that because of the medical costs, my dad had to work two jobs and limit his career goals and enjoyment of life. I remember my parents' joking about how I'd have to make a lot of money some day to pay them back for this sacrifice.*

*"From the beginning, I had the sense that I was the person responsible for all the family stress, and that I was obligated to repay this somehow. As an adolescent, my major career goal was to make enough money to buy my parents a house, even though I knew that would not set things right. There was nothing I could do to repay them for the pressure and stress that I had brought into their lives."*

Both of Paul's parents were Adult Children, although neither became alcoholic. However, the family dynamics were no different from those of alcoholic parents. They simply continued to play out the dysfunctional scripts of their own childhoods. When you are an Adult Child issues of control, inability to know what normal is, unhealthy boundaries and limit setting, need for approval, inability to make decisions, low self-worth, poor problem solving skills, inability to listen, inability to play and shame will gravely interfere with the ability to parent effectively. The inability to express feelings, issues of control and unhealthy boundaries were all prevalent and hurtful to Paul.

*"My dad's stepfather was an alcoholic. He was a harsh disciplinarian, uncaring, and mean. My father was always being blamed and always felt responsible as a child for everything that went wrong. He picked up that way of dealing with children and passed it on to my sister and me. I had this sense that I was obligated to him for the sacrifices he made for me. At the same time, I felt angry at not having had a choice. I relieved that guilt by overworking to try to deserve some good things."*

Paul's mother's father was also an alcoholic.

*"My mother grew up bringing buckets of beer home for her father and raising all of her siblings. My mom had learned to worry and avoid conflict. She also had chronic health problems, and she would attack me as being heartless and cold-hearted when she felt I wasn't empathetic enough about her problems."*

Paul was confused early about boundary issues. He wasn't taught to have an appropriate sense of who was responsible for what. His parents were unrealistic in their emotional and social expectations of him. They held him responsible for their feelings and their adult problems.

*"Everyone was worrying about someone else's feelings and discounting their own. My mother would feel sad and worry about something going on with me. Rather than see that as my mother's sadness and worry, my father wanted me to be different so she wouldn't feel sad or worry. No one wanted to take responsibility for their own problems — they always blamed someone else."*

As Skip had done, Paul would come to find that chronic illness played a significant role in his eating patterns. Because of his illnesses, he was often encouraged to eat to regain his strength.

*"When I was seven, my sister and I stayed with my mom's parents for a few weeks. When my parents came to pick us up, they were shocked—we had both gained considerable weight. My grandmother had given us large dishes of ice cream at night to keep us from missing our parents and also to reward us for being well behaved. At this point food had become not only necessary for my health but also a reward and a soothing substitute for emotions."*

Paul attended Catholic school until the fourth grade, when his family moved from the Midwest to California.

*"The school was run by nuns who were great at instilling guilt and reinforcing the idea that children had to be responsible. We were even taught to feel guilty for feeling shame! We had to bring money for orphans and were told to pray at any free moment for the suffering*

*souls. When we were caught talking in line, we were told souls were suffering in Purgatory because we were not praying to get them out.*

*"I felt miserable about moving. And my parents only made things worse by letting me know that they were leaving home, family, friends, and jobs to go to California just because of me."*

Paul believed that his family moved to California because of his health. This only added to his guilt. It also inappropriately gave the issues of his health and food a lot of power.

A healthy family might also have made the same decision to move. But in a healthy family the parents would have taken responsibility for the decision. In Paul's family the adults were unable to do that. Instead they chose to hold their young child responsible for whatever went wrong from then on.

Guilt was burned into Paul's chest — a guilt that he understood all too clearly he'd never be able to get rid of. Like many COAs, he found that, no matter what he did it wasn't going to be sufficient. He would never be able to be enough or do enough for his parents. In time food would become the only thing that symbolically allowed him to feel *"full," "substantial," "worthy," "enough."*

When the family moved to California, Paul began to attend public school.

*"Again I was the outsider, trying to figure things out, trying not to make mistakes that would lead to embarrassment and family shame. I avoided competition, except in math. I was really quick with flash cards, so I'd compete in that area because I knew I could succeed. Sports competition was out of the question because I was not good enough.*

*"When I was in fifth grade, I had whooping cough and was out of school for several weeks. I remember coming home after my first day back and having a-peanut-butter-and-jelly sandwich and a glass of chocolate milk to unwind from the stress of the day. That became a pattern, and I began to gain weight. When I got to the point where I*

*needed 'husky boy' clothes, my mom began to express concern about my weight."*

Eating after school is common for most children, but Paul was aware that he was eating in response to stress. The other issue was that his mother was going to try to control this part of his life.

Paul learned quite young that he could use his frail health to avoid doing physical activities that his parents wanted him to do. While his poor health made guilt a major theme in his life, he found that food could be an answer to his confusion and pain. At times he was able to vent his anger by using his poor health to his advantage.

*"When my parents wanted me to fish, play Little League, or go to a social function, I would get sick to avoid it. I was scared of social situations. I was afraid of how I was supposed to act. I was angry that I was to go to please them. I was angry that they were always trying to control me."*

Paul said he also played jazz and rock music very loud to deal with his anger. What he understood clearly was that it couldn't be expressed directly.

Paul and his sister got along fairly well. There was some competition, because Paul easily got A's, while his sister had to work hard for her B's. But she was the one family member with whom he tended to have a healthy relationship.

*"I felt relief that there was someone in the family who didn't want me to parent or take care of them. I could feel good about my achievements with her and not worry about having to discount them to avoid hurting her."*

As in many alcoholic families, mealtimes were stressful. Children with eating disorders often describe the need to eat all they can as fast as they can — and to get away from the table. Anorexics describe feeling so tense at mealtimes that they could eat very little. They would pick at food, push it about their plate, but eat nothing. Some children, often overeaters, describe not having any specific dinnertime and feeding themselves all evening long — potato chips, ice cream, macaroni and cheese — all starches and sugars.

*"We generally ate our meals together, and they got pretty heated at times. To me, they were the great myth of what the family was supposed to be but was not. Mom controlled conversations to avoid conflict between my dad and me, while we chafed at the bit to do battle and raced to see who could eat the fastest. This became a habit for me — eating quickly without savoring or absorbing the food."*

Paul was socially isolated for the most part while growing up. Although he usually had one close friend, that friend was often as lonely and isolated as he. Together the two would create their own fantasy world in which to play.

*"My pattern was to find other outsiders and fuse with them. In some way I would live vicariously through them, especially if they had more of a social life. I would gain access to social events through their friendship.*

*"In general, school was a place of stress. There were the straight-A students, but I was always felt below them. Socially I felt out of it with most groups. I felt I didn't like what other people did for fun. Having gone to Catholic school, I was embarrassed by the open sexual behavior of the other students, and I didn't feel comfortable at weekend drinking parties. What I enjoyed doing, I did alone. I just felt strange and different."*

Paul's illnesses kept him home a great deal, increasing his sense of isolation.

*"I never felt as if I fit in; I was always trying to adjust to getting back to school. I got used to working at home alone on schoolwork and then reading, or going off into fantasy, or watching television out of boredom. I was creating my own way out."*

Paul continued his pattern of isolating himself and eating. He would gain weight and then go on a diet. His parents would comment on his self-control, but then he would return to his old eating habits and the weight would come back.

Paul had been six feet tall from the time he was a freshman in high school. Being tall, he tended to look *"big and husky,"* but not obese. But food had become his major focal point, and he perceived himself as *"fat."* However, pictures taken during his childhood show a youngster perhaps ten to fifteen pounds overweight, and in high school, he was about fifteen to twenty-five pounds overweight. But because of his parents' constant responses and comments, Paul perceived himself as fat and that something was wrong with him because of his size.

From the second grade on, Paul had a distorted body image, much like Felicia, whose story follows. He was overweight, and by high school he would be a compulsive overeater and would remain so. While fifty pounds was the most weight he would gain, his whole life was preoccupied with food and body size.

Although Paul's parents may have been trying to be supportive by acknowledging his self-control, they quickly undermined this by being critical, emotionally distant, and blaming. Therefore he placed little value on receiving attention from them.

*"Whenever the weight returned, it was back to dieting and feeling fat, disgusting, weak, unfit, undeserving, undesirable, and scared that I'd be fat forever, scared that I would gain more weight.*

*"My childhood was mostly about fear and shame. I was always so frightened of possible conflict. I also felt I was responsible for my parents' terrible inability to be happy."*

Paul lived in fear of taking on more and more guilt. He was already carrying an enormous burden — the happiness of his entire family. This was exacerbated by the shame he felt around the role of food in his life. The burden became expressed in his body size.

## FELICIA

Age: 41
Mother: Alcoholic
Father: Alcoholic
Additional Dynamic: Incest victim
Birth Order: Youngest of two
Raised: Texas
Socioeconomic Status: Upper middle class

**FELICIA:**

Although both of Felicia's parents were alcoholic, she did not recognize that drinking was a problem. Because her family life had all the trappings of material success, she assumed her parents' focus on drinking was *"normal."*

*"The days in our house focused on cocktail hour, which began promptly at 5 P.M. On weekends and holidays drinking began earlier, but 'never before noon.' The air was filled with tension at all times, but I could never put my finger on what was wrong. I guessed it was something wrong with me."*

Looking back now, Felicia is able to see that the family was clearly alcohol-centered. Her parents were constantly preoccupied with the anticipation of drinking or actual drinking. The message was clear — the day began at cocktail hour. The kids were regarded as a *"duty."* They were attended to physically and materially, but emotionally they were abandoned.

The alcoholism in Felicia's family was covert as it is in the families of many Adult Children. Felicia is the type of Adult Child who often says, *"It wasn't that bad."* In her case, both of her alcoholic parents were in the early stages of chemical dependency. The term 'covert alcoholism' is often used to imply that the consequences are less tangible. But Felicia was responding to the alcoholism long before the signs of chemical dependency became blatant.

It is my belief that alcoholism always affects children negatively, whether the parents are in the early, middle, or late stages of chemical dependency.It is often denial that reinforces one's perceptions of covert or overt alcoholism. Felicia would clearly suffer from her mother's Adult Child issues and her chemical dependency; from her father's chemical dependency; and from her maternal grandfather's sexual molestation of her.

There is no such thing as "It wasn't that bad." The hurt and loss in this family are tremendous. Felicia's denial allowed her to minimize the effects of being raised in her family. It allowed her to avoid the pain.

Felicia's mother also came from a family with two alcoholic parents. In addition, her father was physically and sexually abusive. Because her mother's alcoholism was not blatant, Felicia was responding as much to her mother's criticism and negativity — all unresolved Adult Child issues — as she was to her mother's drinking.

Felicia's mother became even more critical and negative after 5 P.M., something Felicia now realizes was a result of her drinking.

*"My mom was a very angry, controlling person. This certainly began in her childhood. And she did have reasons to be angry with my dad. He was very passive and didn't listen to her. He also acted as if he didn't need her, and all my mom wanted in her life was to feel needed. All I wanted was to at least be heard. I never was."*

This generational cycle repeats itself not just physically, but emotionally. Both Felicia and her mother become alcoholic, both focused on food and body image, and both were starved for love and attention.

Felicia's father wasn't very accessible while she was growing up. Through some shrewd financial investments he started his own real estate business, which was very prosperous. His work consumed most of his time. Cocktail hour began as soon as he got home from work.

Felicia feels that the only things with which her father was able to connect, with any sort of intimacy, were alcohol and food. Her father was overweight, and Felicia's mother was always trying to control his food intake.

*"Overeating was a way to be like Dad. He was always sneaking food, and my mother criticized him constantly for this. Then I stepped into his shoes. I had finally discovered a way to be like Dad and not like Mom; to connect with Dad and to disconnect and distance myself from Mom."*

Felicia's eating patterns would come to be a struggle in response to control by her mother and abandonment by her father.

With hindsight, Felicia now sees that overeating, mimicking her father's behavior, was a way of bonding with him. Overeating was a wonderfully hostile response to her mother's controlling behavior. Eating, when her mother was trying to control Felicia's intake, was power.

Despite her father's unavailability, Felicia kept trying to get closer to him, to connect with him, but she didn't know how. She kept thinking that there was something wrong with her.

*"I wanted to be like my dad. He seemed like a better choice than my mom. At least he was rational and funny. Mom was always so serious and so negative, judgmental, and critical. She was always trying to control Dad. I tried to protect him, but I failed. I tried real hard at everything, but I was never enough."*

The notion of limited supply pervaded Felicia's family life.

*"Was there enough vodka around for Dad's martinis? Enough bourbon for Mom? Enough money? Enough time for me? Enough love?"*

Unfortunately there wasn't enough attention and demonstrated love for Felicia to feel good about herself, so food became her fix.

Felicia says repeatedly that she was never good enough. She was never good enough to get her mother's approval or her father's attention. In time she would find food to be the only solace for the emptiness in her life. She would also discover that she could never eat enough to fill herself up. Her need could only be filled by the overt love and attention of her parents.

Felicia's mother was a housewife. Felicia grew up with a sense that she was always in her mother's way. She also felt a constant sense of disapproval from her mother.

*"I just wanted her attention, and she was always too busy! She had to get food ready.*

*"My mother was also a perfectionist. She was preoccupied with doing everything right. Nothing was ever good enough for her. I remember my mother coming into my room and pulling clothes out of my drawers and then telling me to clean up my room. I felt as if nothing were mine, that at any point I would be subjected to close scrutiny and made to feel inadequate."*

Felicia was living in a family where she was emotionally abandoned. By age six this vulnerable, needy child was being periodically molested by her grandfather.

Felicia and her sister were sent to live with her mother's family — although her parents knew they were alcoholics — for some weeks when her father became seriously ill and needed to be hospitalized. During this visit her grandfather sexually molested her. For the next six years Felicia's grandfather would come to town one or two times a year. He would *"help the family out"* by taking Felicia places. He continued to molest her on these outings. Felicia remembers little of what happened when they were together, but she does remember the fear, shame, and humiliation she felt.

Eating disorders are not just a frequent response in Adult Children of Alcoholics, they are also common among survivors of sexual abuse. Food — compulsive overeating, binging, and starving — meets the same emotional needs when one is the child of both an alcoholic and sexually abusing family, and the likelihood of an eating disorder occurring in such a case is even more pronounced.

Felicia already understood there was something wrong with her. She knew she seemed to be a constant problem to her parents — that, basically, they didn't want to hear from her. She couldn't go to her parents and tell them about the molestation; her parents had sent her to her grandfather's in the first place. Her grandfather was someone she was supposed to love. Felicia's response to the incest was to be compliant and to quickly pretend it didn't happen. She shut down emotionally: Don't think. Don't feel. Just eat.

It was shortly after this that Felicia began to love sugar.

Felicia's parents were very good about providing for her materially, and at the age of seven she turned to horseback riding as a way of winning attention and praise. She would compete in riding events, often for candy bar prizes. It was at this time that she began to get fat.

*"I usually won the races I competed in, and I brought my trophies home — on my body. I got the praise I was hungry for, but I felt as if the hugs were for what I did, not who I was."*

In addition to being an excellent horseback rider, Felicia was a very good student.

*"Overall, school was always a positive experience for me. I did well, and my parents approved. We all had high expectations for me. I was a year younger than the other kids in my class, so socially I was immature. But my grades were good and seemed to be all that was important."*

Felicia was learning that looking good and performing well was what her parents valued. The more she became conscious of that, the more she felt ignored and nonvalued. She was starving for love, but she felt as if she were simply a decoration for her parents. In her conflict to get love and approval, she would continue to perform, but she also sabotaged the *"looking good"* with overeating.

Felicia spent much of her time alone, riding. When she wasn't practicing for a competition, she would ride her horse out into the woods, then find a place to sit and read. She was most comfortable by herself. This was not a sign of self-acceptance, but one of isolation based in fear, a lack of acceptance, and shame.

In Felicia's family the alcoholism was more subtle because trauma was the not yet blatant. Nonetheless, she was experiencing abandonment on a chronic basis. Her emotional needs were being consistently ignored as a result of her parents' alcoholic personalities. Also, she was repeatedly molested by her *"trusted"* visiting grandfather during these years.

Although isolation had become a way of life for her, by the time she entered high school Felicia began to feel the pressure to be like other kids. It was during her senior year in high school that drinking became a part of her social life. She and one of her friends would go out on a regular basis and *"party."*

*"Alcohol and food was the glue that bound our friendship. She was my drinking buddy, and I was hers. By the time I began college, most of my friendships revolved around using alcohol and pot. I was too scared and too much in control to use LSD or other heavy drugs. Alcohol was 'okay.' But I was not okay when using it. I began to be scared that I might have a problem."*

# THE ROLE OF FOOD

Food often plays a very significant role in the lives of children from alcoholic families. It can offer solace to the child who is feeling hungry for love or attention. It can be a friend for the child who feels isolated and alone. A child who develops an eating disorder often substitutes food for the intimacy that is lacking in the family.

However, when these children become overweight, they can find the issues of growing up in an alcoholic family doubly difficult. Self-esteem erodes even further, and self-loathing increases. The child feels the shame twice over — both for the alcoholism in the family and for his or her *"ugly"* body.

Overeating is another way of *"stuffing"* your feelings, something Children of Alcoholics learn to do at an early age. The child may wish to be *"invisible,"* but the overeating is also a cry for attention. As one Adult Child puts it, *"It's a way of killing yourself with food."*

Anorexics may be trying to become less and less visible in order to hide from the inner pain. They may be reacting to the lack of control in their lives, and food intake becomes the one area in which they have some power.

There is also the problem of never feeling as if you're good enough. Becoming anorexic is often a striving after perfection — the perfect weight, the ideal body image. Unfortunately, perception of one's body usually becomes distorted.

The withholding of food may also be a form of punishing one self for being *"bad."* In fact, both overeating and starving can be forms of self-punishment. Bulimics struggle between the two. They flip flop between being out of control in their use of food to comfort and punish and being overly controlling in seeking perfection — the way they present themselves to the world.

In recovery, you have to be able to identify the role that food — or lack of food — has played in your life.

**Role of Food for Skip.** In both childhood and adulthood, food was Skip's best friend. Food was solace. It was nurturance. It helped to anesthetize the pain. But it was also a source of added shame.

**SKIP:**

*"People stared at me; I couldn't fit into chairs. The way I felt about my body, the way I felt about me, just increased my sense that something was wrong with me. I had absorbed all the uncomfortableness of my family in those four hundred pounds."*

Felicia says that feeling fat was a symbol of her shame. For Skip, being fat was the symbol of his shame. Here is a two hundred and twenty five pound ten year old boy; four hundred pounds by his late teenage years. Skip is screaming for help! But his family is so frozen in silence, the only way he or his siblings can speak is through their overeating — and still they are ignored!

*"Prior to my recovery, eating was always secretive. I would eat mainly at night, nonglorious food like peanut butter and bread, bacon and eggs. My secretiveness with food also extended to stealing food from friends' refrigerators, eating off other people's plates as I carried them from the table, eating things I rescued from kitchen trash bags.*

*"Privately I ate to fill myself and quiet my pain. Publicly I ate in a manner that would allow me to avoid attention from other people. I would eat moderate helpings, a salad, no dessert. I would be as invisible as possible. I felt so unworthy in my life that I had to counter any rightful healthy attention I could receive. Then, privately, I would counter that positive attention with negative feelings about what I was shoveling in my mouth.*

*"Even when I was an adult and rapidly losing my weight, my sneakiness continued. I would be at a dinner party and I'd find a reason to leave the table and sneak into the kitchen. I'd find a spoon, get to the freezer, find the ice cream, open it up, gulp down large tablespoons, put the lid back on, clean up the spoon, and wipe my hands because ice cream can often be messy. Then I'd calmly return*

*to the dining area without the other guests being aware of my be-*
*havior.*

*"Throughout all this, I was constantly trying to lose weight. Every*
*month I'd start a new diet, it would last from three days to two weeks.*
*I was obsessed with this constant yo-yoing. It was a very effective tool*
*for avoiding myself, which is what I had been trained to do."*

Many people with eating disorders become as addicted to dieting
as they are to eating. But the dieting is just another attempt at control
— one that is usually doomed because the emotional component of
their addiction is not being adddressed.

**Role of Food for Gloria.** Gloria's eating disorder occurred so
quickly that she has little memory of that time. Her inability to
remember is part of being so removed from her feelings, as well as
the disorientation and confusion that is created by starvation. In
retrospect, with therapy she is aware of feeling that if she ate food she
would cease to be; food would suffocate her.

**GLORIA:**

*"I never thought about food until the crisis was on me. I do know*
*my mom was very careful about our eating. At school I was teased a*
*lot about the strange foods in my lunch box. The other kids always had*
*peanut-butter-and-jelly sandwiches on white bread. I had health foods*
*and whole wheat bread. I would get angry with my mother for being*
*so different and making me feel so different.*

*"Also, my dad and grandfather often told me I would get fat and*
*never get a husband if I kept eating so much. I always liked food, but*
*I didn't carry extra weight. All I knew was, I was doing something*
*wrong."*

Gloria was fighting for her life, but, ironically, in doing so she was
also killing herself. She wouldn't eat because she was afraid that if
she did, she wouldn't know herself. She had very little sense of her
wants or her feelings — it wasn't safe to know them. Yet she literally
hungered to find herself.

*"It wasn't until I began to 'diet' that I began to obsess about being thin. It began by my eating very little, and by eating in a very ritualistic way. I would forbid myself all the foods I loved and would exercise compulsively."*

At the onset of her anorexia Gloria, who was 5'6", weighed one hundred and five pounds. Within six months she was down to seventy-four pounds. She lost her body hair. She lost the fat pads on the bottoms of her feet. She was too weak to walk. She suffered from muscle pain. And she was so severely dehydrated that her skin became chapped and broken, resulting in scars. Gloria was in desperate need of help.

**Role of Food for Paul.** Paul chronically felt left out, alone. As with Skip and Felicia, he never felt he was good enough. In addition, he felt totally responsible for his family's unhappiness. Finding no way to feel good about himself, he made food his best friend.

Compulsive overeaters develop a love-hate relationship with food, and a self-hate relationship lies in the nurturance and solace that food provides. It helps to take the eater's pain away. The hate relationship develops because the food becomes a source of shame. It represents a loss of control and powerlessness that feeds an already deep-seated shame.

**PAUL:**

*"Can a bowl of ice cream be your major sensual experience of the day? For me, ice cream became a tool for self-nurturing. Food was a comforting friend, a sexual friend, that deadened the feelings of stress, anxiety, worry, perfectionism, anger, shame, guilt, and embarrassment. I could relieve those tensions with soothing foods."*

While Skip disassociated from his body, Paul was very focused on his body.

*"As a child I was sick and weak and warned that I'd have a 'chicken chest' if I didn't learn to breathe better through my asthma attacks. When we got to California I remember feeling embarrassed*

FOOD ADDICTION / 45

*about taking my shirt off or wearing shorts because of my pale skin and flabby upper body. Swimming lessons were painfully embarrassing and frightening.*

*"As I gained weight, much of it was in the thighs and buttocks, so buying pants became very traumatic. I always had to buy large-waisted ones with wide legs. And then I had to try them on to see if they were cut full enough. So now I was self-conscious about the lower part of my body, too. To top it off, I developed breasts because of the fat."*

Every fat child has stories of shame about clothing. If shopping can be avoided, it will be. Clothing styles are a part of fitting in, an essential element in belonging. Fat children can't wear stylish clothes. Skip's mother bought his clothes at an outlet that sold uniforms.

For adolescent boys, competing in sports is almost a rite of passage. Any boy who dislikes athletics and is not very developed athletically struggles to some degree with his self-esteem and image. Being overweight creates even greater difficulty in this struggle.

*"I felt physically incompetent in sports because of my weight. Early on I withdrew from competition, so I did not develop any skills. That gave me an ongoing self-definition of 'fat kid' in PE. It was also how the coaches and other kids saw me. Showering in the gym was horribly embarrassing."*

Teens differ in the timing of their sexual development, but they all agonize to some degree over what is right for them. Feeling anxious, confused, and fearful is a natural part of the process. But the COA has an even greater struggle because of mixed messages regarding sexuality. Adding a distorted, negative body image to one's emerging sexual feelings creates even more confusion and fear.

*"Sexually, I felt unattractive. Food helped me over the lonely weekends, while simultaneously making me feel even more undesirable. I was an awkward loner who already felt self-conscious with girls. The weight just added to my negative self-image. My sexual*

*fantasies focused on forcing girls to have sex. The idea of some girl wanting to be sexual with me never entered my mind.*

*"I'd practice playing basketball, volleyball, badminton, and tennis — but I practiced them alone, except for school PE classes. The one good thing was that I was tall. When I felt good, I would see myself as tall, thin, strong, and limber. But when I felt bad about myself, I'd see my body as fat, dumpy, and weak. The confusing part was that my head said I was fat whether I was or not.*

*"Growing up in my family gave me a painful and scary view of the world. Food became my only means of escape from the feelings that view produced."*

Paul's food and COA issues are similar to Skip's and Gloria's. But Skip's compulsive eating resulted in obesity and Gloria's in anorexia. Paul was a compulsive overeater who internalized an image of being fat and not good enough that would become part of his yo-yo cycle of dieting.

**Role of Food for Felicia.** Despite her mother's careful restriction of her diet, Felicia got very mixed messages about food. Still, her problems with food did get her attention — and that was the important thing.

**FELICIA:**

*"Food was love. Food was attention. Food was a way to connect with my dad and break away from and rebel against my mom. Food was the answer. Food was the solution. Food was also a friend.*

*"My mother controlled my food. My sister could eat cookies, peanut butter, and ice cream, while I could not. She could have hamburgers and hot dogs. I got only the meat. At the time I couldn't feel anything, but I now know that I felt deprived, as though there was never enough of anything."*

Felicia got the attention she wanted. But it was negative attention that sliced away at her self-esteem.

*"The same mom who controlled my diet also fed me whenever I
was sick, happy, proud, sad, angry, or even just uncomfortable. She'd
always say, 'You must be hungry. You need to eat. With a full stomach,
you'll feel better.' Eating, not eating, gaining weight, losing weight
— anything and everything about food got me attention. With food I
was the center of the universe. I got the attention I craved."*

To be fed as a response to all one's needs, whether physical or
emotional, makes it difficult for anyone to differentiate hunger from
other bodily signals. Felicia was primed to see food as the answer to
all of her unspoken needs.

The issue of control is major for all ACOAs. For Felicia, control
and food were all bound up together.

*"My childhood relationship with food was all about control. My
mom controlled everything I put in my mouth, or at least she tried to.
I didn't learn to control or manage my own food. All I learned was
how to rebel, how to sneak, how to be dishonest with her and ultimately
with myself. And I felt such shame, even then."*

Felicia's shame reflects not only her perception of her body as *"not
right,"* but also her dishonesty and low sense of self-esteem. Not only
does this create problems for Felicia around food, it also teaches her
to not trust her own perceptions. She learns that she cannot trust others
to meet her needs. To get what she wants, she has to manipulate and
deceive.

Compared with Skip and Paul, Felicia was closest to an average
body size. Although she felt fat, she was only somewhat overweight,
not obese.

*"In high school, I felt fat. I realize now that feeling fat was
synonymous with feeling insecure and lousy about myself. Feeling fat
had little to do with what I looked like or how much I weighed. Feeling
fat was the symbol of my shame."*

Food was also a solace for her shame and humiliation about the
incest. Food was her friend at a time of much fear, shame, and
loneliness.

Food played an early role in the dysfunction of these COAs. Although some people with a childhood eating disorder attend to it during their youth, for most, treatment and/or recovery doesn't occur until adulthood — if at all. When food addiction begins in adulthood rather than childhood, it usually fills the gap left by the cessation of another primary addiction, such as chemical dependency or workaholism.

Felicia found she needed to get sober first before she could deal with her issues around food. Skip recognized his chemical dependency only after recovery from his food addiction. Gloria recognized her food addiction at age fourteen — only to be confronted with the symptoms of yet another food addiction in her twenties. One addiction often masks another, and one addiction often replaces another. In these life stories, three of four people were adults before they could recognize and actively address their food addiction.

# ADULTHOOD AND RECOVERY

## SKIP

Age: 40
Compulsive overeater
Occupation: Psychotherapist
Recovery Process: Self-help, therapy

Skip continued to live at home after he graduated from high school.

**SKIP:**

*"For the first few years after high school, I made no attempt to work. My parents silently accepted my being there. My brothers also stayed at home, but they both worked. Finally, when I was twenty-three or twenty-four, I ventured out and got a volunteer job as a teacher's aide. I didn't believe I was worthy of any pay."*

Food continued to be an answer for Skip. Very little changed in his life during these years, aside from increasing loneliness, sadness, and shame. Then, when Skip was twenty five, his father had heart surgery and died of complications resulting from the operation.

*"When my father died, I initially feigned remorse, but that lasted only a few moments. Then I felt an incredible sense of freedom, a glimmer that I was normal, I wasn't awful, that I had self-worth. I began to realize I had strength. Suddenly I felt important in my family. I planned the funeral. I settled the estate. I took care of the bank accounts. At my father's funeral, my uncle mentioned to my mother that she might need to make some provisions for me regarding my care. But now I was helping to take care of the family."*

Skip's isolation and weight were so apparent, that his uncle assumed he would need to be provided for financially. To the outsider Skip's inability to function was apparent. Yet until his father died, nothing was ever said. Skip's father had been given tremendous power by his family members. But the moment his father died, Skip immediately reclaimed his power.

Unless there is some type of outside intervention, it usually takes an event as powerful as the removal of the source to create change. Yet even then many people have such a deep-seated sense of helplessness that they may be immobilized and unable to respond as Skip did.

It was as if Skip could find no identity, no value in himself, as long as he felt his father's presence. His response was to numb all of his feelings, to kill himself slowly with food. The larger he became, the greater became his need to remain isolated; he not only had to respond to his family's dysfunction, but to the deep, internalized shame he experienced because of society's view of fat people.

*"After my father died, it was as if his toxicity died, too. Somehow my inner child was reconnected with my Higher Power. I had the sense that I was no longer terrible. My father's constant silence had given me a clear-cut message — he hated me. I compounded that by eating and putting on weight in order to feel hateful.*

*"After his death, however, I began to realize that I didn't need food the way I had in the past. After seven months, I had lost over one hundred pounds. Without my father's constant presence, I was able to get a true sense of myself. For the first time I knew that my body wansn't representing to the world who I really was."*

Skip got a job working at a children's home. Two of his co-workers, both male, offered him positive role models of unconditional acceptance. He continued to lose weight. After working there for four years, Skip left and took a part-time job working for a nationally based diet center. It was through this job that he saw the benefits of counseling.

*"I got a lot of affirmation from my class there, but eventually I had to leave because I wasn't comfortable with their system any longer. I continued to work in the child-welfare field and began two years of*

*Gestalt training. Through this, I went into therapy with one of the counselors from the training."*

By this time Skip's weight had been drastically reduced. On the other hand, his drinking had increased. This is not a surprising progression. First of all, Skip is biologically at high risk because the sons of alcoholic fathers are more likely to become alcoholic than any other identifiable group of people. Second, without a recovery program for an eating disorder, people often replace one addiction with another. Skip was involved in a healing process, but it wasn't an active recovery program for his food addiction. By placing himself in a non-toxic environment, he was growing. He had healthy, caring people in his life. But he had not yet dealt actively with his shame. All the repressed feelings of his childhood were still there to haunt him.

*"I was feeling better and beginning to succeed. But I was also beginning to drink. I was continuing a lifelong pattern of abusing myself and also sabotaging my career success. I even flirted with suicide on occasion by drinking and driving. Another time, I took both alcohol and pills, hoping to die, but wanting it to be seen as an accident. I was going through a real inner struggle. Finally I crashed. It was then that I entered a treatment program for co-dependency and alcoholism."*

A therapist at the treatment center identified the alcoholism, although Skip was initially very resistant to the label.

*"I felt it meant that I wasn't in control, that there was one more thing I had to give up, that I was wrong, and even worse, that I was like my dad. Yet the facts were there — I was clearly self-destructive in my drinking.*

*"The woman therapist who confronted me about my drinking also played a significant role in helping me struggle through my resistance. I knew something major was happening at this point because, for the first time in my life, I believed that people truly loved me for just being me. I was feeling unconditional love. In the beginning, I'm sure I continued my sobriety for her. This was not romantic love I was*

*experiencing. It was the realization that another human being truly found value in me, and I didn't want to do anything to mess that up."*

Six months after Skip was sober, and after doing a great deal of work on his own, he began to attend AA meetings. Later on he also began attending Overeaters Anonymous meetings. In both cases he continued to feel out of place and very self-conscious.

*"I didn't feel as if I were good enough to warrant the help of others."*

Dealing with his food addiction proved much more difficult than dealing with his addiction to alcohol. Yet it was in OA that Skip felt an identification more quickly. After some time in this process, he started to attend ACOA meetings. All three groups continue to be a part of his recovery program.

Although self-help meetings have been integral in his recovery, Skip first accepted and surrender to his dependency in an inpatient co-dependency program. Since then he has participated in psychotherapy and also in reconstruction therapy. The reconstruction workshops he refers to are usually a therapy environment in which a group of people work specifically on co-dependency issues. This is usually an intense therapy experience of working together daily over several days (often three to eight days). Role playing and psychodramatic therapy techniques coupled with group process create an intensely cathartic experience that facilitates inner healing. It was there that Skip finally focused on his anger.

*"Anger was the feeling that frightened me the most. My own anger was by far the most difficult and most important feeling I had to 'own' for my recovery. Owning my anger was the only way I could reclaim my childhood.*

*"Expressing anger was difficult for me because I'd learned very early that it wasn't safe to talk about anything. The rules in our house were: 'Don't talk. Don't lose control.' I had only heard my parents fight once, and then it was a very moderate argument. I didn't believe that I had the right to be angry. I wasn't worthy. I thought I had to*

settle for the little I had. In order to work through my anger, I had to reclaim my child from my dad.

"Today, recovery means taking care of my inner child. It means recognizing my many feelings and my needs and nourishing them with attention and respect — not with food. It means reintroducing little Skip to my mother, who has begun her own recovery process. Finally, I'm beginning to get the maternal nurturing I needed and deserved as a small child.

"Other Adult Child issues I've had to work on are control and powerlessness. Eating became the only way I could keep busy and avoid myself, since I thought I was so terrible. Nowadays, without my food dependency, I am not able to feel as bad. Without food, I am not overly controlling. I am learning to face the good things about myself rather than feeling self-hate. Without my food, I lose my main incentive to think strictly in terms of black and white. My life now has meaning beyond merely dieting and binging.

"I've managed to stay connected with my mother and my sister. My sister and I are still close, and she too has begun a recovery process.

"Today, I operate a great deal from feelings. I do what I want to do. I now understand that I am important, and that my own needs have to come first. My life is balanced between work, play, solitude, and friendships — my family of choice. In any twenty-four-hour period, I usually have some contact with all those areas. If I miss any of those parts of my life, it tends to be play, but generally I have a balanced life.

"My body image is where my last real pieces of work have been. I feel great sadness for the stress I have put on my body. I also have a great regard for my body for 'staying with me' and helping me survive. My body and little Skip are very connected, and I find it very important to keep expressing my love and appreciation of them. I've even allowed myself to have some cosmetic surgery in the last few years. It's taken such a long time to give myself the attention I deserve.

*Every day now I'm grateful and happy for myself and my body in some way or another."*

---

# GLORIA

Age: 26
Anorexic
Occupation: Copywriter
Recovery: Therapy

---

When Gloria was fourteen, her anorexia was so completely out of control that many people openly confronted her parents, particularly her mother, about how sick Gloria looked. One day Gloria saw a television report about anorexia and identified herself. She then went to her mother, telling her what was wrong and asking her for help. She asked her parents to put her in a treatment program.

**GLORIA:**

*"I remember becoming rapidly and horribly unhappy with my diseased life. I didn't understand what was happening to me or why. I wanted very badly to be well, and I was very upset with the whole thing. I also knew I couldn't do it on my own — I was way out of control. I knew that the only way I could get better was with the help of my family.*

*"I asked to be taken out of my home and put in a program run from a hospital. It took my family many visits to different doctors to find the therapist who really saved my life. Although this occurred before there was much public awareness of eating disorders, my parents did find a therapist who was an expert in the field."*

In spite of their dysfunction, Gloria's parents ultimately had the ability to respond to the fact that their daughter was dying. Gloria said her mother had been angry with her for months for not eating, but that she'd seen Gloria as being willful. Yet pride, fear, and ignorance did not get in the way once they thought they had a diagnosis for what was wrong — anorexia.

Although Gloria would consistently see her therapist on an outpatient basis for the next two years, she quickly responded to treatment. *"I immediately liked this therapist. I saw him two times weekly and then once a week for over two years. I was so sick that I missed school from December through March, but I felt hope. I was silent for a long time in my sessions. I didn't know what to say. I didn't know there was anything inside of me. But he talked to me and I began to eat for him. He told me I had to."*

Gloria's therapist was a wonderfully safe person for her. She remembers a trust exercise he once did in which he picked her up and set her down.

*"I was willing to let him touch me. I let him pick me up. But all the while I knew he was going to drop me. I waited for him to drop me. And he didn't. I was astonished — he didn't drop me!"*

Gloria was learning about safety, about trust. In many ways her therapist became a surrogate father. Within six months her physical state was stable. However, she has never regained all of her muscle strength, nor the fat pads on the soles of her feet. She can still see scars when her skin is cold and chapped. Her hair has never been as full as it was.

After completing high school, Gloria went on to college. At twenty-six, she has spent nearly all of her adult life in college. For the past two years she has been a copywriter in an advertising agency. Gloria was very young when she began her recovery. At the age of fourteen, however, she lacked the years and the emotional and mentall resources to experience the emotional recovery she would later desire. Although the therapy during high school literally saved her life, she would need to address many more issues in her young adulthood.

*"When I began college I was still thin, fearful of being fat, and had difficulty gaining weight. But in my junior year I was under so much stress that I began to overeat.*

*"Food was never an innocent pleasure for me. There was always the fear of overeating. And now that's just what I was doing. I clearly ate to punish myself. I wanted to punish myself for all the negative things I was feeling about myself — anger, hurt, pain. I would eat alone when no one else was home. I'd take the phone off the hook. There was this ritualistic feel to it all. Now I was Lord and could eat as if I were Henry the Eighth or an Amazon queen."*

This compulsive binge eating was a signal to Gloria that her eating disorder wasn't over. As with any addiction, recovery was an ongoing process. Gloria would need to deal with her recovery issues on a continuing basis.

*"I realized that I had to abandon the dreadful cycle of guilt and punishment: that I had to reject self-abuse. For me, part of this healing has meant strengthening my friendships with older women, working out my issues with the other women in my family, learning to love myself as a woman, and realizing my own strength. As both a Catholic and a recovering Adult Child, I still had vestiges of the saint syndrome: 'One must be all things to all people.' This was certainly reinforced by the role women played in my family."*

Gloria needed to learn to love herself as a woman and to realize her own strengths. Eating disorders are often a feminist issue because many women in our society base their self-image on men's perceptions and value of them. At this time in our history, *"Thin is in."*

Culturally, women are defined and learn to define themselves by their body size and physical attractiveness. For many women, feeling fat is often equated with the belief that one is horrible and worthless. Although men can and do suffer from food addictions, they are not so quick to build their self-esteem solely on body size. They also create value around athletics, job status, and material possessions.

One of the main issues Gloria has had to deal with is her old need to feel *"smaller"* than a man, if only physically.

*"While this is just an old habit for me, it is still hard to break. I feel at peace with myself, with my own intellectual and emotional*

*powers now. But it's hard to get rid of the idea that the thinner one is, the lighter one feels, the faster one moves, and the more graceful one appears. When I'm involved with a man, I still eat less than I normally would, even though the man will usually say that I could stand to gain some weight.*

*"It annoys me that eating is still a 'problem' for me. However, I am much less hard on myself now than I've ever been. If I eat too much, instead of loathing myself, and calling myself a stupid pig, I talk to myself in a soothing manner. I forgive myself and try to figure out why it happened."*

Gloria's old sense that if she doesn't stay extremely thin she'll cease to be is becoming much weaker. It's an old habit, an outworn point of view, based on overemphasizing the superficial aspects of her self-image.

*"Taking care of myself is a relatively new idea for me, and one that I am working on to make a healthy new habit. When I was young I used to test my endurance in lots of small ways. For example, I'd leave the car window wide open on a cold night and let the icy wind whip my face numb before I'd close it. Now I take along gloves in sixty-degree weather, just in case I get cold. Another way I take care of myself is to eat three meals a day instead of one.*

*I'm working on a number of issues now:*

- *Self-care — truly taking care of myself.*
- *Respect — having real regard for my own intelligent, heart-felt choices.*
- *Self-reliance — learning to believe in and rely upon myself.*
- *Trust — learning to trust my feelings and judgments and to trust other people.*

*"Two years ago, at work, someone showed me the twelve questions that help someone know if he or she is an Adult Child, I immediately answered 'Yes' to all of them. I've always been looking for balance. 'All or nothing' behavior has been my norm. I've always had trouble*

with personal boundaries. And I've always been a sponge for the energies of others.

"So much of my life I had no sense of my own space. I was hardly in my own body. I had trouble keeping my own secrets. I would tell people my secrets to purchase intimacy. I've never been malicious — only pitiful. Being an amoeba describes me as well. I easily merge into others. Recently I've been learning to feel and be separate from others. Now I can set healthy boundaries.

"I'm also on much better terms with my issues of control and powerlessness. My entire life I've struggled with my feelings of powerlessness. Rigid control was my only answer. Today I speak my feelings — no more self-distrust. Today I have a sense of me. As I connect with others more and more, I'm finding my own strength. And I'm also finding strength through my love of nature and the arts."

Gloria has been starving for validation and attention, as is the case with so many other COAs. And, as with the others in this chapter, food was an attempt to meet those needs. For Gloria, depriving herself of food was a cry for help that symbolized her emotional starvation.

"I am seeking to find the strength to stand alone, but not be isolated; to know who I am separate from others. I'm learning self-respect and how to provide my own sustenance. In my next love relationship with a man, I hope not to be so pliable, so good, so forgiving, so ready to care at all costs. For years I could not be intimate. But lately I've been too ready — still moving from one extreme to the next, from a stone to a blade of grass.

"I'm continuing to work on acknowledging and showing my strengths, on admitting my full worth."

# PAUL

Age: 43
Compulsive Overeater
Occupation: College administrator
Recovery Process: OA, Al-Anon

Paul began attending junior college after he graduated from high school. During this period he became more and more aware and resentful that his father was trying to find his own identity and worth through possible accomplishments of Paul's. Paul deliberately chose a college path that was not as apt to lead to a high-paying career by majoring in sociology. Later, when he received his bachelor's degree and then his master's, he deliberately did not attend graduation ceremonies in order to deny his father the opportunity to gloat or take any credit for this achievement. Although Paul's anger may not have been readily apparent to him, it was close to the surface.

Up to this time Paul had been a social isolate. He usually had only one friend at a time. He tended to pick peers in crisis, focusing on their lives instead of his own. He continued this pattern when he became romantically involved, marrying a woman who was a practicing alcoholic. She also had three children and had just left a violent, battering, alcoholic man.

**PAUL:**

*"I could protect her. It gave me something to focus on. It gave my life meaning. I was comfortable with the fear and the excitement of impending negativity. However, within months of our wedding her drinking was way out of control. I felt like a failure. At the time we married, I was at a low weight; but within months I started eating again."*

Paul's marriage was at least as chaotic as his family's home life had been. After their child was born, his wife began having extramarital affairs that he knew about.

*"While we were married, I constantly grazed (nonstop picking and eating) through the painful times of betrayal, feeling worse and worse about myself and the weight. Frequently the only pleasant times in our house were spent planning and preparing meals. But the meals themselves were battlegrounds. So at times I expressed my anger by withdrawing from food and meals. Other times I ate to stuff my anger.*

*"The eating was also hidden. Besides grazing all day, I would stock up on soothing things for nighttime and eat alone while my wife was out."*

Paul was beside himself. He lacked the skills and the selfworth to do anything but accept his lot. Again he was left feeling that, no matter what he did, it wasn't right. As always, food was his ally, literally his only friend.

Paul and his wife finally divorced — at her initiation and his compliance. He got a full-time job working for a food vending machine company. This is as suicidal a move as an alcoholic getting a job as a bartender.

*"I was driving around with a whole truck full of chips, candy, and other junk food. My anger and resentment with work problems or my life came out in the truck. Now, instead of waking up from a daze in front of the refrigerator, I was waking up from a daze in the front seat of my truck, surrounded by candy wrappers.*

In time, Paul's ex-wife became sober and suggested that he try going to Al-Anon.

*"What made me take her suggestion was not so much her recovery in AA as my own pain, powerlessness, and feelings that I was going insane. I felt very little connection between what I did and what was happening in my life. I began to realize that being 'nice' would not bring people who cared about me into my life. But I didn't know that I had any other choice.*

*"What I learned through Al-Anon had to do with self-care. I discovered that I first had to be nice to myself before I could draw people to me who were kind."*

Paul was in such pain, and so lonely and confused, that he was willing to listen to what others said — and it seemed okay. Within six months he began to confront his problem with food.

*"I could no longer lose weight or control my eating. Twice a doctor had told me that I was in danger of bringing on diabetes because of my obesity. He said I had to lose weight. I realized that I was killing myself with food, and I knew that that was insane.*

*"So with the three catalysts — Al-Anon, which encouraged my self-love enough to make my eating habits appear crazy; the vending route, where the food stealing and binging made me realize that I had lost control; and the visits to my doctor, who said clearly that my eating was killing me — I had to find help. I turned to another Twelve Step program: Overeaters Anonymous. This time, no authority figure sent me. I went on my own. It meant I had enough self-esteem to be able to love myself enough to do that."*

Through Al-Anon and OA, Paul began to deal with both his overeating and his ACOA issues.

*"The first issue in recovery for me was self-care. I gave myself acknowledgments for each step of progress I made — for being abstinent that day; for making it through the day with some sense of serenity. It became important to me to do kind things for myself: feeding myself an attractive meal, taking a long hot bath, walking in the rain or on the beach. It felt like letting the kid have a place to come out in safety. It also felt like letting the real adult come out in safety while parenting the child."*

Paul also had to deal with the conflicting loyalty issues common to children growing up in dysfunctional families.

*"The rule of not talking about 'negative' stuff outside the family made me feel as if I were being disloyal when I first entered OA. I stopped Al-Anon for six months, hoping I could do just one program*

*at a time. But then I started feeling crazy about family and relationship issues again. So I concluded early on that, for proper self-care, I need both programs each week to remain stable. With them both, I can generally tell when I am hiding from life through work, sleep, or whatever.*

*"It's important for me to realize that my recovery must be my priority. I can no longer allow people-pleasing or parent-pleasing responses to bring me down enough to turn to food again. I need to act on my own behalf on the issues, whether or not my parents understand or support me."*

Paul has found that self-care and self-acceptance mean learning to accept and love his own body, something he was never able to do before.

*"The self-care stage involved a lot of body work so that I could learn to love myself with whatever body I had. I would stand naked in front of a mirror, saying that I loved my thighs and my butt, parts of my body I had never liked because that was where I always gained the weight. I learned to take someone shopping with me so that I'd stop picking out clothes that were too big — I needed help to stop thinking of myself as fat. By including that person, I was also breaking the isolation and secrecy I'd grown up with. Women started noticing me and approaching me, and I began to think that I might be sexually attractive, which was very hard for me to accept at first. It was a completely new way of looking at myself."*

Another area Paul realized he needed to work on was honesty and forgiveness. He had spent years hiding his eating and feeling terrible about himself for it.

*"I had to learn to avoid grazing while preparing and cleaning up after a meal. Initially I set a time limit on my meals to avoid overeating. Eventually I could become less strict with myself because the honesty and forgiveness had healed so much of my self-loathing.*

*"I know that when I start slipping back into my old patterns, I never 'get away with it.' Even if the weight doesn't shoot up right away, my*

*sense of honesty is affected, and the emotional and spiritual parts of the disease kick in. That's when the old self-critical, condemning, perfectionistic ACOA has to start getting honest again — but gently. At times I tell myself, 'I will not eat, no matter what.' At other times I need to quiet the critical part and say, 'My job is to love my Higher Power. To love Paul. All else is a gift.'*

The next issue Paul had to come to terms with was *"normalcy."*

*"I'd always felt different from other people. I now realize that I have a disease that makes me different. By accepting the disease, I have actually learned how to be with people, how to express myself in groups more freely, how to initiate relationships and maintain intimacy. I no longer have to hide out to survive. Just because I can't eat like normal people doesn't mean I can't learn the social skills required to work, achieve, exercise, and love like other people.*

*"I've also learned to deal with the issue of making mistakes. I've learned to acknowledge my mistakes without condemning myself or having to beat myself. Before, when I made a mistake, I became the mistake, and I attacked myself or gave up in despair. I believed that if I couldn't do something perfectly, I wouldn't do it at all."*

Adult Children often struggle with perfectionism. It's common to see them trying to do recovery perfectly and when they realize that's not possible, castigating themselves and even giving up in futility.

*"Now I see that I set too rigid a standard for myself. I'm just setting myself up to fail. If I think that I can control all of my food issues once and for all and never slip again or get sloppy about my eating habits, then I lose the part of the process that is mine — the footwork in the present."*

Paul is recognizing the concept of *"staying in the here and now"* in recovery. He knows he has to take responsibility for himself in the present and not project into the future or obsess on the past.

Because recovery with food addiction cannot be the *"all or nothing"* approach that recovery from chemical dependency demands, the struggle over doing recovery *"right"* is even more difficult for people with an eating disorder. Once they learn that even if they're less than perfect, they're still okay, then they'll be able to live with less fear and a greater willingness to include others in their ongoing recovery.

*"My current issue is trust. It's taken seven years in recovery to make it a focused process. I have to trust that I can have an answer that may not always work the way I want it to, but that this is all right. I have other options. I can ask for feedback from others. I can look for help from my Higher Power. The decision is still up to me. I can make a choice about abstinence and live with the outcome. And if it doesn't work, I can decide to change what I'm doing instead of giving up."*

Both Al-Anon and OA have played an important part in Paul's recovery.

*"I've not been able to do this with just one program. However, with two it's easier to find a balance with my shifting compulsions. Now I can maintain my recovery day to day, rather than switching to a new compulsion.*

*"As a child, my parents were unable to give me the love and support I needed. So I intellectualized and ate my feelings away. In recovery I have learned to value myself and my feelings. I've learned to choose people in my life who enjoy and love that balance.*

*"Now, instead of avoiding risk taking or doing whatever others tell me to do, I've learned to trust my decisions about my life and my judgment on how much risk taking is safe.*

*"Sometimes I have to pretend that everyone I love is dead in order to decide what is best for me or what I want. At other times I think of myself as my own child so I can balance my nurturing for myself with what I give to others. These trusting, loving skills show up in how I'm dealing with food, because food mirrors my feelings. This is one way my Higher Power helps me learn balance.*

*"The trust seems to lead to hope. While I don't know what is next in recovery, I trust my path and the higher force that is unrolling it before me. And I trust me."*

## FELICIA

Age: 41
Compulsive Overeater, Bulimic
Occupation: Account executive
Recovery Process: AA, therapy

Felicia's eating patterns continued through college. Shortly after high school she went to business school and moved out of her parents' home.

**FELICIA:**

*"My roommate — an anorexic nursing student — and I had an apartment. We ate toast with mounds of butter and cinnamon sugar, and then we'd starve ourselves. I'd binge and sneak peanut butter, ice cream, and cookies. I'd often steal food out of the refrigerator at night, hoping she wouldn't notice."*

Felicia's primary choice of binge food has always been ice cream and cookies — the foods her mother offered her sister but not her, and her father's favorite binge foods as well. Alcohol also became more and more important in Felicia's life. For her, drinking was synonymous with eating.

But drinking had brought a twist to Felicia's eating disorder. When she began to drink regularly, as a senior in high school, she also frequently became sick and would throw up. She quickly discovered that, after the initial distaste, she felt relieved.

*"After I'd thrown up a few times, I found that if I drank enough, I could just get rid of it by vomiting. I'd just go do it and then use mouthwash—I learned early on how to keep my clothes clean during it. I'd discovered a new secret. It didn't take me long to realize that I didn't have to drink to throw up. Vomiting was also the answer to my*

*chronic overeating. I could be totally out of control with eating, yet control my weight the entire time."*

Although, many compulsive overeaters have been secretly purging for generations, Felicia's purging took place before bulimia had the public recognition it has today.

Compulsive overeaters experience powerlessness and a sense of being out of control, but purging restores some sense of control. Unfortunately this only helps to keep the eating disorder hidden and never dealt with. Not only is this psychologically dangerous, it can also be life threatening if repeated vomiting ruptures the esophagus or the stomach and causes hemorrhaging.

Felicia saw herself as obese when in reality she was not. Most of the time she was generally twenty pounds heavier than the perceived norm. Occasionally this would climb to thirty to fourty pounds over the norm. But whatever her weight might be, her relationship to food was always unhealthy. Her use of food had prevented her from learning a healthy way of expressing her feelings. In fact, it had created greater isolation and the need for secrecy in her life. It gave her a false sense of nurturance and satisfaction. And it fed her already existing shame. But when she became bulimic as well, she pushed all of of these problems into overdrive.

This is when Felicia became engaged to Jack. She starved herself down to the thinnest she had ever been as an adult. And she moved back home for a month until they were married.

*"I was a bundle of nerves while I was staying with my parents. By this point I was sneaking food, starving myself, drinking alcohol nightly, and doing something else I never told anyone about—wetting the bed. I was such a wreck that the doctor prescribed Valium. I was loaded when I got married, but I was thin."*

In her marriage Felicia was seeking to fulfill the social aspirations of her socioeconomic background. She had found a well-educated husband; she worked and took night classes at a community college; she partied to show life was fun, and she became a mother.

Food was still the central dynamic in Felicia's life. However, after she got married, she and her husband also began a pattern of drinking every night. As is common with so many people with eating disorders, alcohol become addictive for Felicia as well.

*"Food and wine were interchangeable for me. Instead of eating late at night, we'd have a few drinks. We got into gourmet cooking and wine tasting. Then I became pregnant, which was a great excuse to eat.*

*"I always felt fat and was always trying to lose weight. My husband didn't say much about it, but I knew he disapproved just by his looks. He would also buy me clothes that were too small. My mother had always bought me clothes too big for me. No one ever bought clothes for the real me. They bought clothes for their fantasy of me.*

*"After the birth of our second child it took me a long time to lose the weight that I had gained. My husband backed off from me sexually. He said I was rigid, too uptight, not playful or sensuous.*

*"He plugged right into my fears that I wasn't enough as a woman, as a wife, as a sexual partner. What hurt the most was that part of me knew that he was right. In reaction, I did what I knew best when I hurt: I ate and I drank and I threw up. I ate and I drank and I threw up. I felt crazy and depressed. I began to realize that I'd lost any of the control over food or alcohol that I'd once had. That scared me.*

*"As our marriage fell apart, I was devastated. The model I'd learned from my parents was that you dealt with pain by using alcohol. I'd never felt this much pain before because I'd never been allowed to feel. Alcohol, at least temporarily, killed the pain. Alcohol became my friend. I was lonely and scared, and I couldn't turn to my family. They had always told me whenever I cried that I was being silly or shouldn't feel that way. And now my worst fear — that I wasn't really enough — had come true. My marriage was ending, and I felt like a failure."*

Felicia and her husband separated. She went back to work part-time and finished her degree in business administration. But her patterns of binge drinking and binge eating also continued. The pressures of school, the divorce, and taking care of two small children made her let go of some of her perfectionism, but Felicia still felt that she just wasn't *"enough,"* as if there weren't enough of her to go around. And, in reality, there wasn't. Felicia had become super-woman. To nurture herself, she ate and drank, drank and ate.

For reasons she didn't understand, Felicia took a course on alcoholism, even though it wasn't a part of her requirements for school.

*"In the class, we had to write about an addiction. I picked food. At this point I went to Overeaters Anonymous and lost fifteen pounds the first two months, but I was anxious and as close to going over the edge as I'd ever been. I was on overload, out of control. OA was working only in terms of weight loss. But once again someone else was controlling my food — my sponsor.*

Felicia was using her sponsor the only way she knew. She perceived her sponsor as an authority figure, as the critical, judgmental mother with whom she'd been in a life long power struggle. A sponsor is a member of a Twelve Step program that you choose to be your mentor, guide, confidante. He or she is a person you share problems and successes with, who can offer feedback or guidance if you share honestly. Until Felicia dealt more fully with her underlying problems, specifically her anger toward her mother, she would continue to have difficulty using a sponsor. Her Adult Child issues were clearly interfering with her getting the most out of a self-help program.

Felicia was having problems letting go and accepting a Higher Power. Because she felt her drinking was "under control," she didn't tell her OA sponsor about it. She had allowed herself a glimpse of her eating addiction, but her denial was greater toward her alcoholism. Before long she found that she could not address her eating addiction without first addressing her alcoholism.

Interestingly, while Skip began to lose weight before discovering he had an alcohol problem, most food-addicted alcoholics need to stop their dependence upon alcohol and drugs before they can adequately address the eating disorder.

But Felicia's tolerance for alcohol dropped. What she was learning in her alcoholism class made her face up to what was happening in her own body.

*"I had been able to write off or rationalize away all sorts of early-and middle-stage symptoms of my alcoholism. But a drop in tolerance meant my liver wasn't working.*

*"Then we had to write a paper on a female alcoholic and discuss our feelings. I was overwhelmed with feelings. The next thing I knew, I was in the kitchen with a carton of ice cream and a bottle of Kahlua liqueur. I looked at them — the food and the alcohol — and I began to cry hysterically. I called a friend who'd been sober for nine months and asked her, 'How do you know if you're really an alcoholic?' I was at an AA meeting the next morning."*

Although her recovery had begun, Felicia still had to deal with the old feelings that were a part of her ACOA upbringing.

*"Taking on the label 'alcoholic' brought with it a lot of shame. I felt as if I'd failed once again. As I started to deal with how lonely I was and how empty I was, I was so overwhelmed with pain that I turned back to food.*

*"I had never lost the food obsession. I had never let go of my mother's critical messages about me and food. I had not surrendered. I had made people, not God, my Higher Power. I began to binge gain.*

*"By the end of year one of sobriety in AA, I had come a long way. I was less anxious, less critical of me and of others, more able to attend to my children, and doing better in school. However, my new drug of choice — actually an old one revived — was clearly sugar."*

Felicia's weight had gone up to one hundred and eighty pounds, and she turned to therapy in order to deal with the bingeing.

*"In therapy I began to address my drive for perfection and my negativism. In AA I had included food as a part of my daily meditation,*

*my daily writings, and of my daily inventory. My AA sponsor and I*
*worked the steps for this food addiction. Yet I had never told anyone*
*about the purging — which I continued to do."*

People often find that they can attend several kind of self-help
meetings. In Felicia's case OA, AA, ACOA, and Al-Anon would all
be appropriate. As many people do, she combined her food and alcohol
addictions and attempted to work on both, predominantly in AA.
Although this may work for some, it's most likely to be successful
only when alcohol is the first drug to be abused. On the other hand,
trying to work on both addictions at once can also feed one's denial
— primarily the denial regarding food issues.

That is exactly what occurred for Felicia. She was now sober, she
knew she had Adult Child issues, she felt a great deal of shame about
her body and eating patterns — yet she was still hanging on to control.
Not all the truth had been acknowledged or spoken. So, as much as
she was making a stab at recovery for her eating disorder, Felicia was
still trying to control her own program. She was discriminating what
she would and would not be honest about rather than surrendering and
being totally honest. She was still externally focused, hoping outside
entities would provide control against her overeating.

*"Aside from periodic OA meetings and using AA to attend to my*
*eating disorder, I also sought out a nutritionist at times, and an*
*exercise coach. But I remained inconsistent with healthy eating and*
*exercising. I would still binge and purge (not yet telling anyone I did*
*so), I still hated my body and was preoccupied with what others*
*thought. I still felt I needed others to control my eating. Yet this still*
*led to my rebelling when they or I put limits on me around food. I still*
*felt defective, a failure, I still couldn't look in a mirror."*

Felicia was a bright, successful career woman who had been in
touch with all the appropriate resources for over five years, OA,
therapy, and AA. But AA was the only consistent resource in her life.
And not surprisingly, recovery from alcoholism was the area in her
life where she was having continuous success. She was alcohol and

drug free. She was more connected with healthy support people. Her self-esteem was growing, and she was experiencing some joy in her life.

Finally, after five years of sobriety, Felicia's denial cracked. Her controlling behavior, her manipulation of people, places, and things, were out of control. She began to have flashbacks about the childhood incest, and she knew she must seek therapy.

*"When I began therapy, my analyst had me do some 'body' work. It meant first seeing my body. All of my life I had avoided mirrors. If I passed anything that showed a reflection, I'd be so anxious I'd nearly have a panic attack. My experience with incest had affected everything that had to do with my body and all that I had done to it. When I looked in a mirror I saw my grandfather."*

In dealing with her shame and anger over the incest, Felicia uncovered a lot of rage. As she has grown more and more in touch with the rage, she has been able to release the blocked energy, to release the shame. The more she remembers, the more she is able to parent her inner child who never received the nurturing she needed and deserved.

But Felicia's anger, shame, and need for control — and her struggle with powerlessness — was not related to the sexual molestation alone. It was also connected with her parental relationships. Felicia found that she couldn't deal with one area without tapping into the other. She also discovered that, until then, she had been controlling her Adult Child therapy.

Once the incest was recognized, once Felicia began to release her feelings safely, her sense of shame lessened and she found greater self-acceptance. This empowered her to address other sources of anger and to see clearly how her anger had fueled her eating addiction.

*"I knew I had to get angry, but I couldn't. I was bound to my powerlessness."*

Felicia had taken a very depressive stance in life. She had used both food and alcohol to provide solace and to anesthetize the pain.

*"I was angry at my mother for controlling me. I was angry at her criticism and her perfectionism that had so warped my values. I was angry at her for trying to make me a copy of her. Angry at her for treating me differently from my sister. Angry at her for not listening! Angry at her for not making me special! For not protecting me! For robbing me of self!"*

Felicia's recovery is still ongoing. After grief work around the incest, her mother became her focus, because the loss in that relationship was more blatant than the loss of her father. It's easier to identify a loss when it's tangible; Mom did this! And she did that! The loss of her dad was more subtle because it came from what he didn't do.

As many ACOAs do, Felicia found it necessary to address only the issues that felt safe. Food had been the most blatant issue, so she began recovery in OA. But it was in AA that she really felt at home. Her alcohol issues were the safest place for surrender to the recovery process. But food, especially sugar, had been her best friend all her life. The deep and emotionally charged issues underlying her eating disorder would need time, patience, and courage to uncover. It took over five years of active recovery from alcoholism before the incest could and would present itself. And it was only after she began to address the incest that she was totally prepared to deal with her issues with food.

After a year of working with the incest experiences in therapy — with continuing involvement in AA — Felicia found that she could be much more consistent in abstaining from sugar. And after not purging for six months, she was finally able to talk openly about it.

*"I am much more loving to myself around food now. I've really done some incredible work — with God's help — in learning to love at least most of my body. I am much less critical of myself than I used to be. Today, I can look in the mirror and enjoy it. I'm like my own teenage daughter — forever looking in the mirror. My body now has sensations I've never felt before. I was always so busy controlling and discounting, I never even knew I was in pain because I could never*

*feel. I missed over forty years of internal sensations. I was constantly focused on the external—the image, the goal, other people's approval and attention. Now I have my body back. I have me back."*

At last Felicia could begin to recognize how much she had neglected her femininity.

*"For the first time I have come to recognize that I had experienced masculine power as abusive. Today I'm reframing that to see the positive aspects of both masculine and feminine power. I see masculine power as competitiveness, as the ability to set limits, to focus on self as well as others, to get results. I see feminine power as softness, creativity, receptivity. I see it as beingness, as process. I want to have access to all sides of me. I particularly need to work on the feminine side — to be more in touch with my intuitions and internal signals. I want to trust me. Up to now, food, alcohol, and my ever-vigilant control had squashed all of that.*

*"I had rejected and abused my physical being. Today I can look at myself and like what I see. I buy pretty clothes, softer clothes, clothes with color. I nurture my body with exercise, massage, and healthy food. With my friends in self-help groups, my sponsor, my therapist, my Higher Power, I believe for the first time in my life that not only will I be okay, but I am okay just as I am."*

# RECOVERY CONSIDERATIONS

## Primary Addiction

Although Adult Child issues are clearly connected with eating addictions, the compulsive eating that results in obesity, bulimia, or anorexia needs to be accepted as a primary addiction. People with eating disorders need to become involved in a program specializing in eating addiction. It may be a self-help group of Overeaters Anonymous, a psychotherapist who specializes in eating addictions, or an outpatient or inpatient eating addiction program.

Eating disorders are abusive to the body and it is helpful to begin with a total assessment of your health to determine a baseline against which you can measure your ongoing physical recovery. Therefore it is important that those with eating addiction receive a physical examination by a specialist in eating disorders. It is necessary to discover whether there are any physiological causes for the obesity. Then the physical consequences of the addiction need to be diagnosed and treated. Once a commitment is made to follow through on such a program, it is possible to pursue Adult Child issues. I have not found it helpful to put a specific time frame around the period that people are in food addiction recovery before they begin Adult Child work. Once a commitment is made to an eating addiction program, I believe one should begin Adult Child work on the issues around one's relationship with food.

## Multiple Addictions

Addictive personalities often have more than one addiction. As you saw, Felicia had an eating addiction and was also chemically dependent, Skip became alcoholic after he began recovery for his eating disorder. Many recovering alcoholics discover in sobriety that they are food-addicted. Food and alcohol often work in a close partnership

— either they are abused simultaneously, or one is used to discourage overindulgence in the other.

It's easy to begin to feel overwhelmed when you have to respond to more than one active recovery program. The most important thing to understand up front is that having more than one addiction is quite normal for people with eating and chemical dependencies. Each one needs to be addressed as primary. Do not try to substitute one recovery program for another. The next thing on the agenda is to pay attention to how Adult Child issues contribute to the addiction and/or influence recovery.

It's very common to compare one's recovery rate from one addiction with one's recovery from another addiction. However, because there are many similarities in the process of recovery, people often negate the differences. Personally, I would hesitate to say recovery from one addiction may be easier than another. Recovery from any addiction is different from person to person — and it is always miraculous. Although much progress has been made with understanding alcoholism and drug dependency as diseases, the public still tends to perceive eating disorders as willful behavior. It is not. In addition, there is a significant difference between recovery from eating disorders and other addictions, particularly alcohol and drug addictions.

For chemically dependent people, abstinence from alcohol and mood-altering drugs is the core of recovery. But critical to the understanding of eating disorders is that those with food problems cannot abstain from eating. One must eat to live. This fact creates an incredible difference for the food-addictive person.

When people recover from chemical dependency they learn to live their life without using any alcohol or drugs to compensate for emotional states. On the other hand, the food-addicted person must learn to live by adjusting to degrees of use of the very thing they're addicted to — food. It's very difficult to regulate the intake of any addictive substance. Food addicts, whether anorexics, bulimics, or overeaters, must rethink what food means to them and then apply that understanding to their lives. They know that compulsive eating and compulsive starving causes them to think, feel, and act in a manner different from *"normal,"* just as chemically dependent people know that drinking or drugging medicates and anesthetizes feelings. Yet chemically dependent people can stop all alcohol and drug usage. Eating addicts must deal with food several times a day. This is a difficult challenge, but recovery is possible, as demonstrated in the lives of these four people.

## Shame

People with eating disorders feel such incredible shame. Often the eating addiction see-saws between compensating for the shame, and creating the shame. It can become a downward spiral. You must remember that there are deep-seated reasons for the disorder, and that there are people who will both understand this and be of help. You are not a bad person now, and you have never been a bad person. What you were was scared, lonely, angry, powerless. One of the most important gifts you can give yourself is the opportunity to meet others who are recovering from eating addictions. They will understand and not judge. And they can offer direction and hope.

## Incest

If the need to control, starve, purge, or overeat is in any way connected withto a response to incest or sexual molestation, the sexual abuse must be addressed specifically. Incest is prevalent in our society, and an eating disorder is a common response. Whatever the experience, believe me, you were not at fault, and you are not a bad person. You don't need to punish or purge yourself any longer.

## Feelings

Those with eating addictions are extremely disconnected from their emotional selves. Most Adult Children struggle with learning to identify and express their feelings. They struggle with fears of what will occur should they show their feelings. But the emotional self of the person with an eating disorder is directly linked to their disorder.

In the process of recovery from food addiction, one must experience emotional recovery. Overeating, starving, and purging are defenses erected to protect one from further hurt and pain. Unfortunately these defenses don't work. Using food to manage feelings may temporarily distort one's perception of the truth, but it cannot alter the truth. Feelings may be disguised, denied, and rationalized, but a painful feeling will not go away until it has run its natural course. Adult Children must talk about their fears of what will occur when they learn to identify their feelings and express them.

Anger is the feeling most repressed in eating addictions. In recovery it is vital to begin to understand that feelings are signals and cues. Feelings are there to help us, to befriend us — not to hurt us. Feelings will not make us go crazy. They can be particularly painful when they're stored away or denied for many years. But it is possible to walk through the pain.

Be open to the fact that you have many repressed feelings. And that you have legitimate things to be angry about. Anger is a natural reaction when one has been hurt. Personally, I don't think it is possible to be raised in a family affected by as much incredible loss as the ones we've been discussing and not be angry. Some Adult Children have more reasons to be angry than others, but all have some anger that needs to be acknowledged to allow for a more complete recovery.

You must face your anger about things that happened to you in the past. Acknowledging anger will not take away all of the hurt, but it does cleanse one's emotional wound and initiate healing. Once you acknowledge your anger at the past, you will be able to experience the whole rich range of feelings in the present. The anger you might feel at the current experience will become clearer, not clouded by anger and issues from the past. Not being able to identify and display anger is the same as denying it.

As we begin to address how our feelings are connected to food, we can begin to recover from the compulsive eating, the starving, and the purging.

## Control

For bulimics and anorexics, seeking control is the central issue. Obesity is more representative of being out of control. The Adult Child must develop healthy concepts about power and control. We often attempt to control people, places, and things — for example, through the image we present to others — or we control our bodies to mask shame or to compensate for incredible feelings of powerlessness. As adults there are choices available to us that we didn't have as children. Any sense of powerlessness we may feel now is often self-imposed.

It will be important to explore what control and power meant when we were children. Without that exploration, a key connection to what overeating, purging, or starving means to us now will be missed. Usually grief work in that area is necessary. After that, putting the past behind us will be vital to recognizing and accepting where our power lies today.

## Isolation

Those with eating addictions have often lived isolated from others. Do not isolate yourself during recovery. Isolation leads to loneliness, to controlling behavior, and to greater shame. You deserve better.

Because eating disorders are so much diseases of isolation and control, I believe that it is paramount that one begins the group process quickly in recovery. You are not the only person with this problem, and the faster you realize that, the faster your shame lessens. A group experience can sound so frightening, but the sooner you try it the better. This is one case where I find that plunging in can be particularly helpful. It can be of great help in learning to relinquish the tight control you've maintained over every aspect of your life.

## Perfectionism

THERE IS NO PERFECT RECOVERY. People who are compulsive perfectionists were usually raised in families where parental figures had unrealistic expectations of them. As children they internalized those expectations, and today they continue to operate on unrealistic expectations.

When they were children, they needed to do things right — *"right"* meaning no mistakes — in order to lessen their fears of abandonment and to get approval. As adults these people continue to attempt to be perfect. This is often reflected in their image of the perfect body. They struggle with self-hate and disgust at not matching this perfect image. And they take it out on themselves in their overeating, anorexia, or bulimia. Until we can come to terms with our common humanity — our right to make mistakes — it is likely that many of us will continue to overeat, starve, and purge.

In recovery, the source of this perfectionism needs to be dealt with so that you can come to terms with the fact that you are enough, that you are of value, that you are special, that you are important.

*"Today I don't eat compulsively, nor do I deprive myself. Most important, I am able to do that without living in fear of myself."*

Compulsive overeater, Adult Child

# APPENDIX

# SELF HELP PROGRAMS AND NATIONAL ORGANIZATIONS

## Specific To Eating Disorders

### Overeaters Anonymous (OA)
World Service Office
P.O. Box 92870
Los Angeles, CA 90009
(213) 542-8363

### Anorexics/Bulimics Anonymous (ABA)
P.O. Box 112214
San Diego, CA 92111

### American Anorexia/Bulimia Association, Inc. (AABA)
133 Cedar Lane
Teaneck, NJ 07666
(201) 836-1800

### Anorexia Nervosa & Related Eating Disorders, Inc. (ANRED)
Box 5102
Eugene, OR 97405
(503) 686-7372

# ARE YOU A FOOD ADDICT?

|  | Yes | No |
|---|---|---|
| 1. Are you intensely afraid of becoming fat? | ___ | ___ |
| 2. Do you feel fat even when others say you are thin or emaciated? | ___ | ___ |
| 3. Do you like to shop for food and cook for others but prefer not to eat the meals you make? | ___ | ___ |
| 4. Do you have eating rituals (for example, cutting food into tiny bites, eating only certain foods in a certain order at a particular time of day)? | ___ | ___ |
| 5. Have you lost 25 percent of your minimum body weight through diets and fasts? | ___ | ___ |
| 6. When you feel hungry, do you usually refrain from eating? | ___ | ___ |
| 7. If you are a female of childbearing age, have you stopped having menstrual periods? | ___ | ___ |
| 8. Do you often experience cold hands and feet, dry skin, or cracked fingernails? | ___ | ___ |
| 9. Do you have a covering of fuzzy hair over you body? | ___ | ___ |
| 10. Do you often feel depressed, guilty, angry, or inadequate? | ___ | ___ |
| 11. When people express concern about your low weight, do you deny that anything is wrong? | ___ | ___ |
| 12. Do you often exercise strenuously or for long periods of time even when you feel tired or sick? | ___ | ___ |
| 13. Have you ever eaten a large amount of food and then fasted, forced yourself to vomit, or used laxatives to purge yourself? | ___ | ___ |

|                                                                                                                                                                                                                          | Yes  | No   |
| ------------------------------------------------------------------------------------------------------------------------------------------------------------------------------------------------------------------------ | ---- | ---- |
| 14. Are you frequently on a rigid diet?                                                                                                                                                                                  | ____ | ____ |
| 15. Do you regularly experience stomachaches or constipation?                                                                                                                                                            | ____ | ____ |
| 16. Do you eat large quantities of food in a short period of time, usually high-calorie, simple-carbohydrate foods that can be easily ingested (for example, bread, pasta, cake, cookies, ice cream, or mashed potatoes)? | ____ | ____ |
| 17. Do you eat in secret, hide food, or lie about your eating?                                                                                                                                                           | ____ | ____ |
| 18. Have you ever stolen food or money to buy food so that you could start or continue a binge?                                                                                                                          | ____ | ____ |
| 19. Do you feel guilt and remorse about your eating behavior?                                                                                                                                                            | ____ | ____ |
| 20. Do you start eating even when you are not hungry?                                                                                                                                                                    | ____ | ____ |
| 21. Is it hard for you to stop eating even when you want to?                                                                                                                                                             | ____ | ____ |
| 22. Do you eat to escape problems, to relax, or to have fun?                                                                                                                                                             | ____ | ____ |
| 23. After finishing a meal, do you worry about making it to the next meal without getting hungry in between?                                                                                                             | ____ | ____ |
| 24. Have others expressed concern about your obsession with food?                                                                                                                                                        | ____ | ____ |
| 25. Do you worry that your eating behavior is abnormal?                                                                                                                                                                  | ____ | ____ |
| 26. Do you fall asleep after eating?                                                                                                                                                                                     | ____ | ____ |

|  | Yes | No |
|---|---|---|

27. Do you regularly fast, use laxatives or diet pills, induce vomiting, or exercise excessively to avoid gaining weight?

28. Does your weight fluctuate 10 pounds or more from alternate bingeing and purging?

29. Are your neck glands swollen?

30. Do you have scars on the back of your hands from forced vomiting?

### Scoring

Five or more yes answers within any of the following three groups of questions strongly suggest the presence of an eating disorder:

Questions 1 to 15: Anorexia nervosa.
Questions 14 to 26: Binge eating.
Questions 12 to 30: Bulimia.

### Getting Help

If you think you may be a food addict, chances are you've kept your fears to yourself for a long time. Asking for help takes courage, but it's worth the risk. Admitting your problem to yourself and to others who share your problem will give you a great sense of relief. This chapter describes several organizations that sponsor support groups nationwide. Try contacting a few of these groups. Get more information on the subject. Reach out. Help is just a phone call away.

Reprinted from The Recovery Resource Book. Barbara Yoder.

# THE ORIGINAL LAUNDRY LIST FOR ADULT CHILDREN OF ALCOHOLICS

## The Problem

The Characteristics we seem to have in common due to our being brought up in an alcoholic household:

A. We became isolated and afraid of people and authority figures.

B. We became approval seekers and lost our identity in the process.

C. We are frightened by angry people and any personal criticism.

D. We either become alcoholics, marry them, or both, or find another compulsive personality such as a workaholic to fulfill our sick abandonment needs.

E. We live life from the viewpoint of victims and are attracted by that weakness in our lives and friendship relationships.

F. We have an overdeveloped sense of responsibility and it is easier for us to be concerned with others rather than ourselves; this enables us not too look too closely at our own faults, etc.

G. We get guilt feelings when we stand up for ourselves instead of giving in to others.

H. We become addicted to excitement.

I. We confuse love and pity and tend to "love" people we can "pity" and "rescue."

J. We have stuffed our feelings from our traumatic childhoods and have lost the ability to feel or express our feelings because it hurts so much. (Denial)

K. We judge ourselves harshly and have a very low sense of self-esteem.

L. We are dependent personalities who are terrified of abandonment and will do anything to hold on to a relationship in order not to experience painful abandonment feelings which we received from living with sick people who were never there emotionally for us. .

M. Alcoholism is a family disease and we became para-alcoholics and took on the characteristics of that disease even though we did not pick up the drink.

N. Para-alcoholics are reactors rather than actors.

## The Solution

By attending Adult Children of Alcoholics meetings on a regular basis, we learn that we can live our lives in a more meaningful manner; we learn to change our attitudes and old patterns of behavior and habits, to find serenity, even happiness.

A. Alcoholism is a three-fold disease; mental, physical, and spiritual. Our parents are victims of this disease which either ends in death or insanity. This is the beginning of the gift of forgiveness.

B. We learn to put the focus on ourselves and to be good to ourselves.

C. We learn to detach with love; tough love.

D. We use the slogans: LET GO, LET GOD; EASY DOES IT; ONE DAY AT A TIME, etc.

E. We learn to feel our feelings, to accept and express them, and to build our self-esteem.

F. Through working the steps, we learn to accept the disease and to realize that our lives have become unmanageable and that we are powerless over the disease and that alcoholic. As we become willing to admit our defects and our sick thinking, we are able to change our attitudes and our reactions into actions. By working the program daily, admitting that we are powerless; we come to believe eventually in the spirituality of the program — that there is a solution other than ourselves, a Higher Power, God as we understand Him/She or by sharing our experiences, relating to others, welcoming newcomers, serving our group, we build our self-esteem.

# PROGRESSION CHART
## Alcohol Addiction

Read from left to right

**EARLY STAGE**

INCREASE IN
ALCOHOL TOLERANCE
SNEAKING DRINKS
URGENCY OF FIRST DRINKS
AVOID REFERENCE TO DRINKING
PREOCCUPATION WITH ALCOHOL
DECREASE OF ABILITY TO STOP
DRINKING WHEN OTHERS DO
GRANDIOSE AND AGGRESSIVE
BEHAVIOR OR EXTRAVAGANCE
FAMILY MORE WORRIED, ANGRY
GOES ON WAGON
EFFORTS TO CONTROL FAIL REPEATEDLY
HIDES BOTTLES
PROMISES OR RESOLUTIONS FAIL
FAMILY AND FRIENDS AVOIDED
WORK AND MONEY TROUBLES
TREMORS AND EARLY MORNING DRINKS
PROTECTS SUPPLY
DECREASE IN ALCOHOL TOLERANCE
ONSET OF LENGTHY INTOXICATIONS
DRINKING WITH INFERIORS
INDEFINABLE FEARS
UNABLE TO INITIATE ACTION
VAGUE SPIRITUAL DESIRES
ALL ALIBIS EXHAUSTED
COMPLETE DEFEAT ADMITTED

**DENIAL**

OCCASIONAL RELIEF DRINKING
CONSTANT RELIEF DRINKING
ONSET OF MEMORY BLACKOUTS
(IN SOME PERSONS)
INCREASING DEPENDENCE ON ALCOHOL
CONCERN/COMPLAINTS BY FAMILY
FEELINGS OF GUILT
MEMORY BLACKOUTS INCREASE OR BEGIN
LOSS OF CONTROL
ALIBIS FOR DRINKING
PERSISTENT REMORSE
CHANGE OF PATTERN
TELEPHONISTS
TRIES GEOGRAPHICAL ESCAPE
LOSS OF OTHER INTERESTS
FURTHER INCREASE IN MEMORY BLACKOUTS
UNREASONABLE RESENTMENTS
NEGLECT OF FOOD
PHYSICAL
DETERIORATION
IMPAIRED
THINKING
OBSESSION WITH
DRINKING
ETHICAL
DETERIORATION

**MIDDLE STAGE**

**LATE STAGE**

OBSESSIVE DRINKING CONTINUES
IN VICIOUS CIRCLES

# THE ROAD TO RECOVERY

ENLIGHTENED AND INTERESTING WAY
OF LIFE OPENS UP WITH ROAD
AHEAD TO HIGHER LEVELS THAN
EVER BEFORE

FULL APPRECIATION OF
SPIRITUAL VALUES

GROUP THERAPY AND MUTUAL HELP CONTINUE

CONTENTMENT IN SOBRIETY

FIRST STEPS TOWARDS
ECONOMIC STABILITY

CONFIDENCE OF EMPLOYERS

APPRECIATION OF REAL VALUES

INCREASE OF EMOTIONAL CONTROL

REBIRTH OF IDEALS

FACTS FACED WITH COURAGE

NEW INTERESTS DEVELOP

NEW CIRCLE OF STABLE FRIENDS

ADJUSTMENTS TO FAMILY NEEDS

FAMILY AND FRIENDS
APPRECIATE EFFORTS

DESIRE TO ESCAPE GOES

REALISTIC THINKING

RETURN OF SELF-ESTEEM
DIMINISHING FEARS OF THE
UNKNOWN FUTURE

REGULAR NOURISHMENT TAKEN

APPRECIATION OF POSSIBILITIES
OF NEW WAY OF LIFE

CARE OF PERSONAL APPEARANCE
START OF GROUP THERAPY

ONSET OF NEW HOPE

GUILT REDUCTION
SPIRITUAL NEEDS
EXAMINED
STOPS TAKING
ALCOHOL

PHYSICAL OVERHAUL BY DOCTOR

RIGHT THINKING BEGINS

MEETS HAPPY SOBER ALCOHOLICS

TOLD ADDICTION CAN BE ARRESTED

LEARNS ALCOHOLISM IS AN ILLNESS
HONEST DESIRE FOR HELP

*REHABILITATION*

— Modified form M.M. Glatt

# DO YOU HAVE THE DISEASE OF ALCOHOLISM?

When considering the possibility of alcoholism, please consider two things: First, the nature of the disease is to trick its victims into believing they can control their drinking. Second, making an effort to control one's drinking is, by itself, a sign of alcoholism. People who don't have an alcohol problem don't think twice about how much they drink. They set a limit and stick to it. If your drinking causes problems in any area of your life with your family, at work, in social settings, emotionally or physically, financially, or with the law, it's worth finding out more about this disease.

Alcoholism strikes one out of every ten people who drink. Not everyone has the physiological makeup to become alcoholic, but anyone who drinks could be at risk. Alcoholism doesn't discriminate. It affects people of all ethnic backgrounds, professions, and economic levels. It is not known precisely what causes this disease, but drinking is clearly a prerequisite. Therefore everyone who drinks should periodically evaluate their drinking patterns and behavior. This test, reproduced with permission of the National Council on Alcoholism, Inc. (NCA), will help you to determine whether or not you have symptoms of the disease. Answer the questions honestly, with a simple yes or no.

|  | Yes | No |
|---|---|---|
| 1. Do you occasionally drink heavily after a disappointment, a quarrel, or when the boss gives you a hard time? | ___ | ___ |
| 2. When you have trouble or feel under pressure, do you always drink more heavily than usual? | ___ | ___ |

|                                                                                                                     | Yes | No |
|---------------------------------------------------------------------------------------------------------------------|-----|----|

3. Have you noticed that you are able to handle more alcohol than you did when you were first drinking? ____ ____

4. Did you ever wake up on the *"morning after"* and discover that you could not remember part of the evening before, even though your friends tell you that you did not *"pass out"*? ____ ____

5. When drinking with other people, do you try to have a few extra drinks when others will not know it? ____ ____

6. Are there certain occasions when you feel uncomfortable if alcohol is not available? ____ ____

7. Have you recently noticed that when you begin drinking you are in more of a hurry to get the first drink than you used to be? ____ ____

8. Do you sometimes feel a little guilty about your drinking? ____ ____

9. Are you secretly irritated when your family or friends discuss your drinking? ____ ____

10. Have you recently noticed an increase in the frequency of your memory *"blackouts"*? ____ ____

11. Do you often find that you wish to continue drinking after your friends say they have had enough? ____ ____

12. Do you usually have a reason for the occasions when you drink heavily? ____ ____

13. When you are sober, do you often regret things you have done or said while you were drinking? ____ ____

14. Have you tried switching brands or following different plans for controlling your drinking? ____ ____

|                                                                                           | Yes | No |
|-------------------------------------------------------------------------------------------|-----|----|
| 15. Have you often failed to keep the promises you have made to yourself about controlling or cutting down on your drinking? | ___ | ___ |
| 16. Have you ever tried to control your drinking by making a change in jobs or moving to a new location? | ___ | ___ |
| 17. Do you try to avoid family or close friends while you are drinking? | ___ | ___ |
| 18. Are you having an increasing number of financial and work problems? | ___ | ___ |
| 19. Do more people seem to be treating you unfairly without good reason? | ___ | ___ |
| 20. Do you eat very little or irregularly when you are drinking? | ___ | ___ |
| 21. Do you sometimes have the *"shakes"* in the morning and find that it helps to have a little drink? | ___ | ___ |
| 22. Have you recently noticed that you cannot drink as much as you once did? | ___ | ___ |
| 23. Do you sometimes stay drunk for several days at a time? | ___ | ___ |
| 24. Do you sometimes feel very depressed and wonder whether life is worth living? | ___ | ___ |
| 25. Sometimes after periods of drinking, do you see or hear things that are not there? | ___ | ___ |
| 26. Do you get terribly frightened after you have been drinking heavily? | ___ | ___ |

Any *"yes"* answer indicated a probable symptom of alcoholism. *"Yes"* answers to several of the questions indicate the following stages of alcoholism:

Questions 1 to 8: Early stage.
Questions 9 to 21: Middle stage.
Questions 22 to 26: Beginning of final stage.

Volunteers at local affiliate offices of NCA can provide further information to help you assess whether or not you have a drinking problem. They can also refer you to services and treatment programs in your area. Check the phone book under "Alcohol" or call **1-800-NCA-CALL** (1-800-622-2255) for the number of your community's NCA affiliate.

# Books by Claudia Black

My Dad Loves Me, My Dad Has A Disease

It Will Never Happen To Me

Repeat After Me

It's Never Too Late To Have A Happy Childhood

Double Duty — Gay—Lesbian

Double Duty — Chemically Dependent

Double Duty — Food Addiction

Double Duty — Sexual Abuse

A complete catalogue of MAC products, including videotapes, note cards and related material, can be obtained free of charge from:

**MAC PUBLISHING**
a division of Claudja, inc.
5005 East 39th Avenue
Denver, CO 80207
(303) 331-0148 • Fax (303) 331-0212